Praise for Baker and Goodman's
A, B, Cs of Author Partnering

"This book is a must-read for anyone beginning a writing project with a partner. It is comprehensive in scope, going far beyond the nuts-and-bolts of who will write what and whose name goes first on the byline. Baker and Goodman provide a solid framework for developing a rich, productive author partnership, including thorough coverage of business and marketing aspects, time management, and handling conflicts. This is practical, valuable advice from experienced, successful writing partners who practice what they preach."

—K. Gaberson, PhD, RN

"I THINK THIS IS A GREAT LITTLE BOOK. I enjoyed reading it. It was easy to read while conveying important concepts and facts. I found the exercises interesting and applicable to more than a writing partnership!"

—J. Rothrock, PhD, RN

"Great go-to book to get started co-authoring."

—C. Gable, BS, RN

"The authors describe the important discussions and logical steps to follow before partnering with another author."

—A. Clark, BA

"The A, B, & Cs of Author Partnering has excellent advice for working with a partner to write a book or an article. It has valuable suggestions that are not always considered. It is well-organized and easy to follow."

—P. Seifert, MSN, RN

"If you are considering writing for publication, this book is a must-read. One person might not have the variety of skills or the time to write, edit, and publish. This book covers it all: contract negotiation, partnership management, conflict resolution, and work-life balance - everything you need to build a successful author partnership and get your manuscript completed."

—D. Herrington, MS

"The authors did a great job and I am impressed by the scope of this work. Partnering with another writer can be the answer to completing a manuscript. The A, B, & Cs of Author Partnering is well-written, and the workbook has great exercises for creating a productive writing partnership."

—N. Girard, PhD, RN

A, B, & Cs OF AUTHOR PARTNERING

JOY DON BAKER
&
TERRI GOODMAN

A, B, & Cs OF AUTHOR PARTNERING

Copyright © 2019 by Baker & Goodman

All rights reserved. No part of this publication may be reproduced, distributed, or transmitted in any form or by any means, including photocopying, recording, digital scanning, or other electronic or mechanical methods, without the prior written permission of the publisher, except in the case of brief quotations embodied in critical reviews and certain other noncommercial uses permitted by copyright law.

Published 2019
Printed in the United States of America
ISBN: 978-1-7345150-0-8
E-ISBN: 978-1-7322535-9-9
Library of Congress Control Number: 2018914869

Written by Joy Don Baker & Terri Goodman
Foreword by: Jennifer Gray, PhD, RN, FAAN
Cover design: *Fresh Design*
Interior design: *JETLAUNCH.net*
Interior graphics with permission from *PresenterMedia*
Author photo: *Simao Ago*

For information:
Baker & Goodman
Watauga, TX
admin@bakergoodman.com
www.bakergoodman.com

TABLE OF CONTENTS

LIST OF FIGURES AND TABLES ix
FOREWARD xi
PREFACE xv

1. ALIGNMENT 1
   1.1. Partner Alignment 2
   1.2. Scope of Project 4
   1.3. Authorship 7
   1.4. Ghost and Guest Authors 10
   1.5. Framework for Alignment 11
   1.6. External Team 12
   1.7. Publication 12
   1.8. Competition and Replication 13
   1.9. Conclusion 14

2. BALANCE 15
   2.1. Work-Life Balance 15
      2.1.1. Values, Functions, and Dimensions 16
      2.1.2. Politics and Burnout 17

		2.1.3.	Motivation 20

        2.1.3.   Motivation 20
        2.1.4.   Recognition 21
  2.2.   Time Management 21
  2.3.   Managing Self 24
  2.4.   Conflicting Obligations 25
  2.5.   Conclusion 27

3. COMMITMENT 28

  3.1.   Types of Commitment 28
        3.1.1.   Personal Commitment 29
        3.1.2.   Continuance Commitment. 29
        3.1.3.   Normative Commitment 30
  3.2.   Influences on Commitment. 31
  3.3.   Statement of Commitment. 32
        3.3.1.   Equality 33
        3.3.2.   Transparency 33
        3.3.3.   Results-Oriented Focus 34
        3.3.4.   Responsibility. 34
        3.3.5.   Complementarity. 35
  3.4.   Behaviors Consistent with Commitment 35
  3.5.   Conclusion 36

4. CONTRACT. 37

  4.1.   Finding Sample Contracts 39
  4.2.   Elements of Agreement 40
        4.2.1.   Author Order and Roles 41
        4.2.2.   Income and Expenses. 42
        4.2.3.   Workload, Representation, and
                       Warranties. 42
        4.2.4.   Partner Disputes and Dissolution. 43
  4.3.   External Team Contracts 44
  4.4.   Conclusion 45

5. COMMUNICATION 46

  5.1.   Communication Styles 47
  5.2.   Purposeful Communication. 48

	5.3.	Communication Tools. 50
	5.4.	Listening: A Means of Communication 51
	5.5.	Bridging the Generation Gap 53
	5.6.	Diversity in Communication 54
	5.7.	Infrastructure 55
		5.7.1. Management Tools. 55
		5.7.2. Meetings. 56
	5.8.	Conclusion 58
6.	**CONFLICT RESOLUTION** **59**	
	6.1.	Resolving Conflict by Leadership Style 60
		6.1.1. Impoverished Leader and Avoidance Strategy 61
		6.1.2. Country Club Leader and Accommodation Strategy 62
		6.1.3. Task-Oriented Leader and Domination/ Competition Strategies 62
		6.1.4. Middle of the Road Leader and Compromise Strategy 63
		6.1.5. Team Management and Collaboration Strategy 64
	6.2.	Conclusion 66
7.	**COMMERCE** **67**	
	7.1.	The 4Ps: Marketing Mix. 68
		7.1.1. Product 68
		7.1.2. Place. 69
		7.1.3. Promotion 70
		7.1.4. Price. 71
	7.2.	Online Systems. 72
		7.2.1. Website and Blogs 72
		7.2.2. Electronic Communication. 73
		7.2.3. Social Media. 74
	7.3.	Conclusion 75

- **8. CREATIVITY** **76**
  - 8.1. Ethics 78
  - 8.2. ADDIE Model 80
    - 8.2.1. Analysis 80
    - 8.2.2. Design 82
    - 8.2.3. Development 82
    - 8.2.4. Implementation 82
    - 8.2.5. Evaluation 83
    - 8.2.6. Time Allocation 83
  - 8.3. Practice Writing as an Artist 86
    - 8.3.1. Pictographic Illustrations 86
    - 8.3.2. Lifeline 88
  - 8.4. Conclusion 90
- **9. CALL TO ACTION** **91**
- **WORKBOOK** **93**
- **REFERENCES** **133**
- **ACKNOWLEDGEMENTS** **149**
- **AUTHOR NOTES** **151**
- **ABOUT THE AUTHORS** **153**

LIST OF FIGURES AND TABLES

Table 1.1:	Ten Key Points for Successful Team Science Collaboration	8
Figure 2.1:	Core Values intersecting with Functional Areas	17
Figure 3.1:	Commitment Scale	31
Figure 5.1:	Ten Steps to Effective Listening	52
Figure 5.2:	Sample Agenda	57
Figure 6.1:	Leadership Styles and Conflict Resolution Strategy	61
Figure 8.1:	Writing Fun - Work Scale	77
Figure 8.2:	Steps to Success	78
Figure 8.3:	Addie Model	80
Table 8.4:	Partner Writing Project (% of Time)	84
Figure 8.5:	Street Sign Image Examples	87
Figure 8.6:	Story Lifeline	89
Table 9.1:	Partner Checklist	131

FOREWARD

In 1989, I was involved in a study at a large hospital related to a computer staffing program for nurses. I had just finished my master's degree in nursing and was teaching in a university-based nursing program. As naïve as I was about university structure and politics, I knew the university rewarded publications and research. Presenting and publishing the findings of the staffing study was an expectation. Disseminating these findings was my first experience in author partnering. Fortunately, my partner was generous in sharing what he knew, and the experience was positive. Next, I wrote research reports with a nursing team of faculty studying spiritual care in nursing. Producing publications was difficult for the team because we did not establish the ground rules before we started. The last six years I have been writing research textbooks with established authors who have had the patience to guide me through the processes of contracts, marketing, and splitting royalties. What you can conclude is that I have been writing with others for almost 30 years. Some experiences were positive and some not so positive. Many painful lessons could have been avoided if this book had been available.

The *A, B, & Cs of Author Partnering* begins with **A**lignment of the members of the partnership, a critical step in determining the compatibility of the partners in important areas such as trust and expected outcomes. **B**alance is described in Chapter 2 as making time to write the product for which the partnership was established as well as making time for relaxation, employment, family, and other necessary components of life. Baker and Goodman provide a visual model of the overlap of professional, interpersonal relationships, work, and personal care. Using questions included in the narrative, the partners can identify their core values, then share and discuss them with one another. Understanding the motivations, values, and competing priorities provides a foundation for the partners to support and encourage each other through the life of the project. It also helps the partners to consider what matters most to them and create realistic deadlines.

The first C in the book is **C**ommitment, Chapter 3. A logical outcome of understanding the values, motivation, and obligations of the members of the partnership is being able to make an informed commitment to the project and each other. Baker and Goodman recommend drafting a formal statement of commitment that specifies details of the partnership, including the responsibilities of each member. Ideally, the strengths of the partnership members are in different areas. When that is the case, the partnership creates synergy that results in a product beyond what the individuals could produce separately.

Chapter 4, **C**ontracts, describes the importance of having a contract for the partnership. Some contracts will include external entities such as agents or publishers. Again, the authors have provided an exercise that elicits discussion among the partners to ensure that all important aspects of the relationship are addressed in a contract. The best contract, however, will be worth little unless the partners can communicate with each other, especially when they disagree.

Communication is the topic of Chapter 5. Four personality types are described along with their preferred styles of communication. Knowing your own type and the types of your partners gives insight into the effectiveness of the communication patterns being used by the partners. Suggestions are provided on how to improve communication. Different tools of communication, such as face-to-face conversation and email messages, can be selected based on the recipient's personality type, the information to be communicated, and time available for a response.

Continuing with the Cs, Chapter 6 addresses Conflict Management. The authors organize the conflict management strategies according to the leadership styles of partners. As an example, a task-oriented leader is more likely to use a domination/competition strategy to resolve conflicts. For me, this chapter provided insight into my conflict management strategies and an opportunity to reflect on the conflicts that I had experienced in partnerships.

Commerce, Chapter 7, considers the realities of marketing the product of the partnership. The product, place, promotion, and price comprise the 4Ps of marketing. Considering these factors prior to finalizing the product's purpose and structure is important. How difficult to invest time and energy into producing a book or article, only to find out that the market is saturated with similar products. The partnership needs to consider the types and numbers of products the target readers already have available to them, how their product will be made available to target readers, and how these potential customers will learn about the product.

Chapter 8, Creativity, counters the business considerations of the previous chapter with the playfulness involved in writing creatively. Partners may have different perspectives on balancing fun and work. To avoid the pitfall of creativity without an outcome, Baker and Goodman provide the ADDIE model to help a writing project move forward creatively.

The strategies described in the first eight chapters will never result in a product without action. Chapter 9, Call to Action, reviews the chapters with a Partnership Task Checklist followed by the directive to write, write, and write. Throughout the book, the authors provided questions and prompts to engage the readers with the material. These same questions and prompts are provided as a workbook at the end of the text. The workbook is designed with adequate space to record your answers, logically structure the partnership, and create an effective plan for writing the product.

There is something here for anyone who is an author, no matter the amount of experience. I find this book provides insights that will guide a novice author as well as new information and thought-provoking questions to refresh the thinking of a more experienced author. The authors have struck the perfect balance between theories and application to the real world by allowing theories and models to structure relevant questions and strategies for building a partnership.

Don't take my word for it, however. Read it for yourself!

Jennifer Gray, RN, PhD, FAAN
Associate Dean, College of Natural and Health Sciences
Oklahoma Christian University

Professor Emeritus
The University of Texas at Arlington

PREFACE

Authors are passionate about sharing knowledge, experiences, and stories to inform or entertain others. The *A, B, & Cs of Author Partnering* introduces a valuable option for initiating and producing significant literature of any type. Although writing a book may be a daunting task for an individual, joining forces with a partner can provide the motivation, focus, and the right mix of knowledge and skill to achieve the dream. Whether communicating the results of a research study, describing an evidence-based project, or penning a book of fiction or non-fiction, partnering with a colleague can transform the desire to write into reality.

Successful partnerships are based on alignment and balance, crafting an agreement that frames and acknowledges each partner's commitment and contributions, collaboration, and effective communication. We address the *who, what, when, where, why,* and *how* that partners should explore prior to undertaking a writing project.

Author partners contribute a diversity of strengths and skills, providing a broad base to address the variety of tasks involved in writing, publishing, and marketing a completed product. Their commitment to one another and to the project keeps them focused on completing their work and experiencing the joy that accompanies success.

Assumptions

Partnerships can be comprised of an unlimited number of individuals who may be geographically distant from one another. For the purpose of simplicity and consistency, we used two partners to represent partnerships of all sizes throughout the book. The content remains relevant regardless of the size of partnership or location of the partners.

The second assumption relates to face-to-face and distant (online) communication among partners. We emphasize the value of face-to-face interaction among partners, especially when developing new ideas, resolving conflict, and celebrating. All these activities can be accomplished effectively from a distance using a variety of electronic tools.

Operational Definitions

The following list of terms with their operational definitions promotes clarity and continuity throughout the book.

- **Product:** The final outcome or result of the partners' efforts; the collective written work; a book (fiction or non-fiction), a scholarly publication (i.e., journal article, research study, quality improvement project, or systematic review, etc.).

- **Project:** The collaborative enterprise encompassing all of the carefully planned work associated with producing the published product.

- **Goal:** Broad strategic direction of the project.

- **Objectives:** Incremental subsets or tactics that support the goal; can be expressed in a sentence beginning with an action verb.

- **Writing Partner:** An individual who creates an alliance with one or more persons to share the work, risks, and benefits of creating a document for publication.

- **Partnership:** As few as two individuals or a large number of authors who collaborate to produce a written product; may include interdisciplinary or international authors.

- **External Team:** Other individuals or companies engaged to assist in completing the project: statistician, publisher, editor, agent, publicist, designer, graphic artist, etc.

Icons

Two icons are used throughout the book.

Indicates an exercise for enhancing comprehension; use the workbook to complete the exercises.

Indicates an external resource for additional information.
Included in the *A, B, & Cs of Author Partnering* are chapters on alignment, balance, and seven Cs: commitment, contract, communication, conflict resolution, commerce, and creativity. The chapters may be read sequentially or independently based on the needs of the reader.

Chapter 1: Alignment

In *Alignment,* we explore the partners' relationship and a process to assure that the content of the project is consistent with the needs of the target readers. The chapter includes exercises for addressing authorship and author order and determining the roles of guest and ghost authors. The exercises are intended to engage partners in an effective process of aligning with one another to achieve success.

Chapter 2: Balance

An effective partnership respects work-life balance to ensure that the partners have the time and support to be productive authors. Whether writing is a full-time or part-time endeavor, partners must incorporate personal relationships and obligations into the planning processes. This chapter includes the influence of values, motivation, and effective time management on partnership productivity, and includes project scheduling, timeframes, deadlines, unique project elements, and negotiating conflicting obligations.

Chapter 3: Commitment

The success of a writing partnership is predicated on the partners' commitment to one another and to the project. In this chapter, we explore partnership structure and function, the difference between *equal* and *equitable*, and transparency. Commitment in partnerships includes a results-oriented focus, responsibility, and complementarity.

Chapter 4: Contract

We are neither attorneys nor legal advisors. The information presented in this chapter is based on our own successful contract development process. Useful contract elements include clarifying the roles of the authors related to the business of writing, the management of finances, and the disposition of the work products should the partnership dissolve. Partners negotiate the division of labor through open, candid dialogue. Elements of agreement may be recorded formally in a contract or documented informally in policy or meeting minutes.

Chapter 5: Communication

Clear communication, including purposeful dialogue and active listening, is essential to the success of a partnership. Written and verbal communication, both personal and official, must be well-managed. Partners must assume responsibility for communicating clearly, especially when the communication styles of the partners differ. Effective communication includes the necessity for bridging the generation gap and using diversity to produce meaningful written works.

Chapter 6: Conflict Resolution

Diversity among partners can create the need to manage conflicting ideas, disparate processes, and different expectations. Effective partners approach conflict as an opportunity to achieve synergy and to produce an outcome superior to any of the original alternatives. Tools for resolving conflict include negotiation, decisive communication, compromise, and collaboration. The goal of conflict resolution is always to achieve consensus and advance the project.

Chapter 7: Commerce

Authors must explore options for publishing their completed work. For books, self-publishing is increasing in popularity, especially since traditional publishers are demanding extensive involvement from authors in marketing their work. Success with either approach requires that authors participate in all facets of marketing and sales, mastering the *4Ps of Marketing* (product, place, promotion, and price). Authors must have a robust marketing strategy that involves, at a minimum, a website and at least one social media platform. For articles, select journals with appropriate target readers. Be diligent in complying with the journal's author guidelines.

Chapter 8: Creativity

Authors in a robust partnership recognize and value one another's strengths and compensate for each other's weaknesses. Authoring challenges partners to think creatively, beyond their everyday experience. Partnering can free a left-brained writer's shadow self to exercise creative right-brain thinking. In contrast, right-brained partners benefit from their left-brained colleague's organized and methodical approach and respect for structure. Creativity also involves attention to the ethical concepts of truth-telling and consistency of voice.

Chapter 9: Call to Action

The A, B, and Cs of Author Partnering is intended to provide the knowledge that will catapult a partnership into action. Dreaming about writing is a first step and producing a finished product requires **ACTION**. Once partners are aligned, committed, and have determined what will be done by whom and when, it is now time to **WRITE**. Do not permit inertia to stand in the way of your published work.

Workbook

Exercises throughout the book facilitate the development of an effective partnership. The Workbook provides tools for completing the exercises.

1

ALIGNMENT

Writing with a partner requires alignment of purpose. Together, partners must ask themselves *What are we trying to achieve?* They must articulate the *why* (purpose) and the *what* (goals) that establish the foundation for the partnership. Partners can explore concepts independently, then collaborate to discuss their ideas, negotiate divergent concepts, and confirm tactics. Collaboration keeps partners from taking parallel or duplicative paths that would inhibit progress.

No project can be fully realized until partners develop trust in one another. Trust implies that there are no hidden agendas and that concerns are discussed openly. Exploring conflicts, either perceived or real, is essential to achieving resolution and reinforcing the goals of the partnership. Maintaining their focus on the purpose keeps the partners on track, and confident as they advance the project. Organizing content and establishing milestones for celebration keep the partners aligned, committed, and enthusiastic.

Partner Alignment

Alignment implies that the partners are *on the same page* while recognizing, respecting, and accepting that each has unique views, priorities, and needs. For example, one partner's family responsibilities may be a priority while another may be interested primarily in the recognition associated with publication. Open discussion about personal and professional motivations, expectations, and perceptions promotes partnership alignment.

1.1 Use the workbook to document your answers to the following questions:

- What do I personally want from this project?
- Why am I here?
- How will the project benefit me personally/professionally?
- How will this project change my life, my work, my family?
- What will I commit to the project?
- What am I willing to sacrifice for the project?
- What do I want to walk away with if we dissolve our partnership?

When both partners have completed the exercise, review the responses together, exploring areas of agreement, discussing opposing viewpoints, resolving disparities, and creating new ideas.

Dialogue among the partners helps to determine if they are compatible and if their individual needs are in alignment with the goals of the partnership. Early identification of challenges (e.g., both partners expect to lead the project and have the final authority) allows the partners to resolve the issues or determine that they cannot work well in partnership.

1.2 Respond to the following questions after deciding to work together. Use the workbook to capture your individual responses, then discuss responses collectively to foster alignment.

- Why do I want to work with this partner?
- What does this partner bring to the table? *(perhaps that I don't, won't, or can't)*
- What do I value most in my partner?
- How do I support my partner when we face challenges (i.e. slow progress, slumps, writer's block, or external pressures)?
- How can my partner support me when we face similar challenges?

Sharing personal goals, desires, and perceptions promotes transparency and alignment by reducing the potential for misinterpretation and misperception. Respecting the diversity among partners is an important aspect of alignment. Partners should listen carefully to one another's ideas and explore all aspects of an issue before making a final decision. Open dialogue provides the opportunity to resolve differences before they can interfere with productivity. During alignment, the partners should commit to a standard that ensures that no conflict will remain unresolved.

1.3 Use the workbook tool to answer the following questions, then share your responses with one another.

- To whom are we committed?
- What role does transparency play in our partnership?
- What steps will we take to ensure transparency?
- How will we
    o demonstrate diversity?
    o demonstrate our commitment to ensuring that no conflict remains unresolved?
    o manage conflicting priorities?

Refer to the responses to the exercises in this chapter when negotiating the partnership contract agreement (Chapter 4). Reviewing the responses reminds the partners of their commitment to alignment, and promotes productive discussion when they encounter hurdles or face conflict during the project.

Scope of Project

Identifying the target readers and asking them what they want and need determines the focus, scope, value, and relevance of the project. For example, the target audience for a novel about nurses might include *avid readers of women's fiction, females 18-years or older who enjoy reading about nurses and their challenges*. The target audience for a research study on sterilization of surgical instruments might include *perioperative nurses, sterile processing employees,* and *infection preventionists*.

1.4 Early in project planning, respond as specifically as possible to the following questions:

- What is the purpose or primary goal of the project?
- What specific knowledge, skill, and/or experience do I bring to the project?
- Whom will this project serve?
- How will the target audience benefit?
- What is the best format to meet the target readers' needs?
    - Journal article: New practice? Solution to a problem? Fill a gap in the literature?
    - Book: Fiction or non-fiction?
- How long should this project take?
- Why am I willing to invest time and effort?

After completing the exercise, review responses together.

Once the partners are aligned on the project purpose and the target readers' needs, they can craft the overarching goal that describes the project's strategic direction or outcome. Then they define the incremental steps (objectives) that detail the scope (breadth and depth) of the project. A description of the scope and content of the project should be immediately accessible throughout the project to ensure that the partners remain focused on the target. The S.M.A.R.T. (specific, measurable, achievable, relevant, and time-bound) framework[1] is a tool to help the partners focus on immediate and long-term goals.

1.5 Using the S.M.A.R.T. framework[1] respond individually to the questions below, share and discuss your responses, then finalize the overarching goal statement for the project.

Initial Goal: *Record the initial or draft project goal.*

1. **S**pecific:
    a. *What is/are the specific goal(s) targeted for accomplishment?*
    b. *Why is the goal personally important? Be specific about what achieving the goal means both to the individual and to the partnership*
    c. *Use the answers to "who, what, when, where, why, and how" to develop the overarching project goal.*

2. **M**easurable:
    a. *Record specifically what the outcome will look like when completed.*
    b. *How will goal progress be evaluated?*

3. **A**chievable:
    a. *What is the partners' shared motivation to accomplish the goal?*
    b. *Are the skills needed to complete the project available within the partnership? If not, will the partners develop the skills or solicit them from external team members?*
    c. *Are the partners' assignments balanced fairly and assigned appropriately, based on the skills needed to achieve the goal?*

4. **R**elevant: *Determine whether each objective is aligned with the project goal. If not, what will it take to adjust them?*

5. **T**ime-bound: *Establish realistic deadlines.*[1]

Edit the Goal: *Does the goal need editing based on the responses to this exercise?*

This exercise should be repeated periodically during the writing process to achieve consensus in identifying key elements and defining and clarifying intermediate objectives.

Authorship

Determine the criteria for authorship early in the project. Avoiding *credit confusion*[2] for authorship requires transparency and open dialogue about who receives credit for the work and how authority, accountability, and responsibility for accuracy and integrity of the work is allocated.[3]

Rose and Anders[4] introduced the concept of *team science* representing interprofessional, cross-disciplinary groups who use large databases for study and analysis to bring depth and diversity to strategies, maintain traction, and move their project forward. (Table 1.1) These team science principles are applicable to all types of literature and to partnerships with any number of authors.

Table 1.1: Ten Key Points for Successful Team Science Collaboration[4]

10-Key Points
1. Familiarize yourself with the team members.
2. Stress open communication and avoid lingo unique to a profession.
3. Determine authorship and author order early.
4. Share team meeting minutes making them readily accessible.
5. Create a process of shared decision-making.
6. Create an environment that encourages the team to function at a high level.
7. Conduct face-to-face meetings as frequently as is practical.
8. Develop conflict resolution strategies early in the partnership development.
9. Create meaningful methods for inclusion of students or readers.
10. Find opportunities to celebrate.

Authorship and acknowledgment represent two distinctly different elements of contributing to a writing project. The International Committee of Medical Journal Editors (ICMJE)[5] recommends four criteria on which to base authorship:

1. Substantial contributions to the concept or design of the work; or the acquisition, analysis, or interpretation of data for the work; AND

2. Drafting the work or revising it critically for important intellectual content; AND

3. Final approval of the version to be published; AND

4. Agreement to be accountable for all aspects of the work in ensuring that questions related to the accuracy or integrity

of any part of the work are appropriately investigated and resolved.[5]

Journals often incorporate or adapt this set of criteria to assist authors in clarifying the appropriateness of authorship. Those who contribute valuable content but do not meet all four criteria should not be listed as authors.[5,6] Authors can demonstrate their appreciation by recognizing the contributors in an *Acknowledgements* section.

Items three and four of the ICMJE criteria are critical. Authors are held accountable for the published material and must be willing and able to address questions related to the integrity of the work.[6,7] Prior to publication, confirm, do not assume, that individuals wish to be recognized to avoid the possibility of a contributor's claim to know nothing about the project, the content, or the authors.

Negotiating to clarify the order and role of authors and documenting decisions early in the planning process provides the transparency that can prevent future conflict. Authors can be listed alphabetically, according to the quantity of contribution, or randomly, such as by the flip of a coin. Any method of author ordering is acceptable if the partners agree. For authors of scholarly works, author order may be an important decision, as professional acclaim is often tied to publishing. Occasionally, a citation, reference list, or index listing will record only the first author, followed by "et. al." meaning the first author may receive more recognition than the other partners.

Decisions related to author ordering should be captured in a written document (e.g., partnership contract, policy statement, minutes) that can be referenced as needed, such as when the editor of a journal questions authorship in a manuscript. Different disciplines may vary in their preferences for the ordering of authors. For example, the senior or sage author may be listed in the last position, with the primary author or principal investigator listed first;[8] other disciplines may list the most senior person as the first author.

For an in-depth review of author order, particularly for scientific writing, read Phillippi, Likis, and Tilden[8] 2018 article "Authorship grids: Practical tools to facilitate collaboration and ethical publication" in *Research in Nursing and Health*.

Every author is responsible for completing writing assignments and coordinating with partners to ensure a cohesive manuscript. Frequent communication among partners provides clarity and keeps the project in alignment. All authors participate in the final approval of the manuscript before it is submitted for publication.[8]

Authors of qualitative and quantitative manuscripts are responsible for participant protections, design, data collection, and analysis. Authors of literature synthesis must establish design review and literature search strategies, then determine the sources for review, data evaluation, and synthesis.[8] Partners authoring both fiction and non-fiction must determine who will contribute what content, then manage the layout of scenes and chapters to produce a single manuscript. The final manuscript should be seamless as if it were written by a single author.

Ghost and Guest Authors

Ghost authorship is generally a contractual agreement in which an author receives monetary compensation for writing someone else's content or story. For example, celebrities who have neither the skill nor the time to write an autobiography employ a ghost author to write the book for them. When the work is published, the owner of the material, not the *ghost author*, is identified as the author. Companies may hire accomplished writers to ghost author their publications. The ghostwriter is not listed as an author in the publication. The published product belongs to the company, not the ghost author. Ghostwriting is inappropriate for scholarly publications which should be written by the investigator(s) of the study or project.[9]

Guest or *gift* authorship describes the inappropriate practice of recognizing an individual as an author who did not contribute to the written work. If an employer, professor, or team leader will approve a writing project only if he/she is listed as an author, the legitimate author(s) should seek guidance within the organization's administrative structure to resolve the issue. The appropriate method for recognizing someone who has supported a writing initiative is in the *Acknowledgements*.

The *guest author* should not be confused with a *guest editor* who is an individual hired to coordinate a special issue of a journal. The *guest editor* is responsible for soliciting and managing authors who will write articles for that journal issue. The *guest editor* often writes the editorial for that issue and may also author one or more articles.

Framework for Alignment

Alignment among partners promotes operating at peak effectiveness.[10] The most damaging scenario for partnership alignment is the absence of well-defined opportunities for consistent communication.[11] Partners must establish a shared vision or direction, then develop performance indicators and clearly-defined goals to promote steady progress toward their objectives. The partners' interdependent roles, mutual understanding, and respect are based on the principles that guide their behavior and the strategies they employ to achieve their goals.

Addressing organizational structure at the outset of the partnership furthers alignment and ensures that partners agree on all aspects of the partnership that affect their outcomes. Success depends upon confirming that the partners' strengths offset one another's weaknesses and that they have the resources needed to achieve their goals.

Griffin[11] highlights five elements that create a framework for system alignment: (a) common destination, (b) clarity on how the system works, (c) supporting processes, (d) marketing opportunities, and (e) trust.[11] For example, system operations for writing a novel or a journal article can include keeping files in a shared location using software such as *Dropbox®* or *Google® Docs*. Creating redundancy by saving documents frequently. Preserving previous versions of the manuscript can prevent disaster should material be deleted accidentally.

Partners working on individual objectives can lose sight of the project as a whole. Creating a dashboard to monitor the milestones keeps partners on track. Use a spreadsheet or organizational tool (*Trello®*, *Kanbanflow®*, etc) to document the progress of journal sections or book chapters and scenes. Markers such as word count or chapter completion highlight milestones to celebrate.

External Team

Completion of a project may require outside assistance and resources. Partners create trusting relationships with a community of contributors and consultants such as a statistician, graphic artist, editor, and publisher who share ideas and perspectives and provide specific skills to assist the partners in achieving their objectives. External contributors' work should be aligned with the partnership's project goals. Acknowledgment of their work can be recognized appropriately in the published work.

Publication

The partners must be aligned on such elements as selecting a journal for an article, seeking a traditional agent and publisher, or self-publishing a book. Self-publishing is rising rapidly in popularity.[12,13,14] Partner who self-publish develop marketing strategies that include soliciting and managing all of the external team members required to complete the project: editors, interior layout, graphic designers, and publisher, etc. Partnering with a colleague can make the complex and time-consuming tasks of writing and publishing easier.

Sometimes time-sensitive events, concerns, or crisis situations require that information be published quickly to meet the immediate needs of a target audience. Traditional routes of publication may not be able to serve this target audience's needs in time. Professional journal editors have printing schedules that may prevent them from providing information as quickly as the audience demands. For example, during the Ebola crisis in the U.S. in 2014, nurses were hungry for useful and vetted information for implementing best practices in patient care. Key government and nursing leaders and other healthcare providers collaborated to discuss the issues, explore the facts, and share relevant information with caregivers by hosting online webinars, blogs, websites, and venues for rapid publication. The in-depth articles and books that followed chronicled the situation, addressed the adjustments made during the crisis, and established guidelines for best practices.

Competition and Replication

Partners creating a new work must explore the competition to ensure the individuality and alignment of their project with the marketplace. They must explore other successful publications that are indicators of target audience interest in the topic, field, or genre to identify the focus and direction of their content and suggest different study participants, characters, plot twists, locales, time periods, and writing styles to distinguish the new product from the competition. In scholarly literature, replication of studies is necessary to validate outcomes and establish best practices. Repeated studies either reinforce practice recommendations or demonstrate that alternative approaches achieve better results.

Conclusion

Establishing mutually supported goals and the order of authorship early in the development of a partnership promotes alignment and allows partners to move forward in concert, negotiating adjustments as needed. Successful partners recognize the value in their diversity, capitalize on their strengths, and compensate for one another's weaknesses. Aligning their project with the needs and expectations of their target readers makes their work meaningful. Partners celebrate milestones and foster a positive environment that provides motivation and momentum for advancing their project.

2

BALANCE

Respect for the rich relationships among partners provides the balance that makes the partnership productive and satisfying. A writing partnership exists within the framework of the partners' relationships and external activities. Partners must acknowledge stressors related to work, family, friends, health, and caring for the spirit and self that can challenge the well-being of the partnership. They must establish a balance that makes the partnership productive and satisfying.[15] In this chapter, the term *work* represents the authoring activity of the partnership to produce the product. *Life* represents activities, commitments, and relationships external to the partnership.

Work-Life Balance

Work-life balance means that partners accept and respect their dual commitment to the partnership and to their personal obligations.[16,17,18] Achieving work-life balance is essential to sustaining motivation and productivity, decreasing stress, and increasing the partners' perception of the value of their efforts to produce their work on time and within budget.

Most individuals want to participate in the decisions that affect their lives. Partners prefer collaborative decision-making to the traditional top-down approach of those in charge determining what is to be done, when, and by whom.[16] They appreciate the freedom to pursue diverse activities such as professional and personal self-development and service to the local community. Partners want to engage in meaningful and ethical work and may choose an option that pays less because it provides opportunities for sharing, hope, and paying forward to society. Partners who determine what is meaningful in life and work remain enthusiastic, maintain a high level of morale, and achieve positive project outcomes.[16]

Values, Functions, and Dimensions

Finding work-life balance requires that each partner explore the six core values: (a) *Sense of Self*, (b) *Achievement*, (c) *Intimacy*, (d) *Creativity & Play*, (e) *Search for Meaning*, and (f) *Compassion & Contribution*.[19] Core values apply to four intersecting functional areas of life: (a) *Work*, (b) *Professional* (career development or service), (c) *Interpersonal Relationships* (couples, family, friends), and (d) *Personal* (self-care, health & nutrition, spirituality). (Figure 2.1).[20,21]

Figure 2.1: Core Values intersecting with Functional Areas

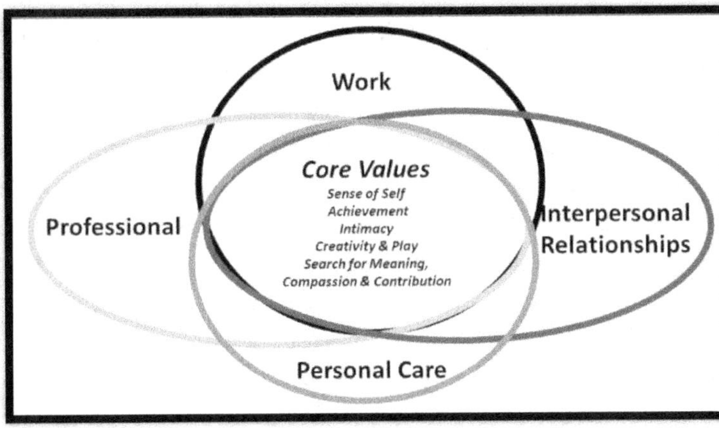

Venn diagram showing overlapping areas: Work, Professional, Interpersonal Relationships, and Personal Care, all intersecting at Core Values (Sense of Self, Achievement, Intimacy, Creativity & Play, Search for Meaning, Compassion & Contribution).

The partners control their work-life balance by determining the dimension level of (a) the *time* they devote to work and non-work activities, (b) the *satisfaction* they derive from the activities, (c) and the degree to which they are *involved*.[22] *Satisfaction* and *involvement* provide a dimension of quality that *time* alone cannot address. Balance among needs is unique to each individual, and a partnership provides an environment conducive to meeting individual needs.

Politics and Burnout

Burnout from undue stress and unmet needs can stimulate self-serving behaviors that disrupt the partnership and severely curtail productivity.[23] This disappointing behavior can frustrate hard-working partners who withdraw psychologically, feeling incompetent and exhausted. Finding ways to prevent burnout and reduce political upheaval through effective, ethical, and positive communication supports the partnership.[23]

Burnout develops when there is a disparity between the individual and one or more of these six factors: "workload, control, rewards, community, fairness, and values".[23] For instance, a partner who does a disproportionate amount of work while the other partner cannot or will not do his/her share is at risk for burnout. Unfamiliar work demands, limited resources, and lack of opportunity to participate in decision-making also contribute to burnout.[23] Burnout increases the potential for a partner to neglect the project or leave the partnership.

Gaining support from friends and family and talking openly about issues can help reduce stress, improve one's outlook, and prevent burnout. Partners should acknowledge their needs and ensure that they are met. Failure to address personal needs can be detrimental to both the individual and the partnership. Seeking help is never a sign of weakness. Partners who are unable to manage stress might consider soliciting assistance from a mental health professional or through an employee assistance program.[24] A strong support system correlates with an aggressive immune response and protection from illness.[24]

2.1 Work-life balance is unique to each person. *What is most important to you regarding work-life balance?* Respond to the following questions and consider sharing the results with your partner.

- If I were to die today, what would I say were the top three **accomplishments** in my life? The list created addresses your personal values.

- From the six **core values,** (a) Sense of Self, Achievement, (b) Intimacy, (c) Creativity & Play, (e) Search for Meaning, and (f) Compassion & Contribution, determine the one most associated or the best fit with each accomplishment listed.

- Record the **functional area,** (a) Work, (b) Professional: Career development or Service, (c) Interpersonal

Relationships: Couples, Family, Friends, and (d) Personal: Self-care, Health & Nutrition, and Spirituality, where each of the accomplishments took place.

- Using the three scales for **dimension levels,** (a) Time, (b) Satisfaction, (c) Involvement, place an X to indicate whether you spent more or less time on each accomplishment related to all work-life activities in which you were engaged at the time.

Relating the exercise to anticipated or future accomplishments assists the partners in exploring their personal *bucket lists,* both for the project and for life.

2.2 Explore your involvement level by responding to the following questions:

- How willing are you to commit the **time** required to achieve the goal?
- Will the work provide a level of **satisfaction** that allows you to make the goal of the partnership a personal priority?
- What level of **involvement** in decision-making related to the partnership activities do you want?
- Are you willing to adjust the **time** that you are involved in other activities that may be preventing you from accomplishing your desired level of **satisfaction** and **involvement** in the partnership?
- What can you give up that will represent little or no sacrifice, to free up **time** for the work of the partnership?

Motivation

Hertzberg's motivational theory, although focused on the traditional workplace, has relevance for partnerships. Hertzberg identified two sets of factors:

a. **hygiene factors** including working conditions, policies and administrative practices, compensation, the relationship among partners, job security, and personal life and

b. **satisfiers** including recognition, achievement, advancement, growth, responsibility, and job challenge.[16,25]

When hygiene factors are aligned with one's personal values, they are considered acceptable, have a neutral effect, and maintain the partner's commitment to the partnership. Hygiene factors are not satisfiers, but if they are *not* met, they immediately become dissatisfiers[16,26] that can lead to frustration and burnout.

2.3 From the lists of motivational factors, hygiene and satisfiers, determine which serve as motivators. Other questions that may help identify the project motivation level include:

- What is going well?
- What values in life are important to you?
- What aspects of the partnership are important to you?
- What gives you the most enjoyment?
- What are the barriers you perceive to a more satisfying partnership?
- Is there someone or something in your life that is stopping you from achieving your highest level of satisfaction?

- How can you convert these barriers to opportunities?
- Who is your writing ally? Who helps keep you on schedule?
- With whom do you need to spend time to further your ideas?[16]

To promote work-life balance, each partner must identify the satisfiers associated with involvement in the partnership and in personal life, then determine how best to ensure that they are met. How partners choose to manage their years, months, weeks, days, and minutes helps them achieve a greater feeling of control within the partnership and in everyday life.

Recognition

Writing can be arduous and time-consuming; therefore, acknowledging each partner's contributions is necessary to foster continued enthusiasm for the project.[27] Recognizing progress reinforces the strengths of the partnership and highlights achievement. Celebrating milestones energizes and motivates the partners by calling attention to their progress. Partners share their favorite parts of the journey with one another, noting what worked well and what improvements might make the next milestone easier to reach.[28] Celebrations are playful and balance the work associated with progress with relaxation and social interaction.

Time Management

Achieving partnership goals while maintaining a work-life balance that may include other employment commitments requires proactive time management. Partners should structure their work time purposefully. They should turn off controllable interruptions such as phone calls, emails, and social media and set aside a specific time to address them.

During the negotiation process with external team members, partners must indicate how and when they are available. Establishing a routine and informing others of one's availability promotes consistency. Establishing standards is effective when partners adhere to the boundaries they set and respond within the designated time frame. Others learn to trust that the partner will not breach that obligation and therefore will wait for the response. Those who expect immediate responses may have to be reminded of the boundaries of your time. For instance, a partner may state,

> "I generally respond to email at least once in a 24-hour period Monday-Friday. While I may respond more frequently, please limit expectations to this time frame."

Ranking the importance of each email, phone message, and social media post helps determine what can be discarded, what must be addressed immediately, and what can be postponed.[24,29] Gilkey's[30] **S.T.A.R.** triage process for exploring and prioritizing email can be helpful.

- **Scan** the inbox
- **Trash** all that can be discarded
- **Archive** relevant resource materials
- then **Respond**.

He suggests that the process for responding repeat the S.T.A.R. acronym.

- **Start** with urgent messages
- **then** move to older ones.
- **Answer** one or two of the tougher messages.

- ***Re-evaluate*** whether there is time to attend to additional ones or postpone for another time.[30]

2.4 For one week, one hour a day, practice off-line skills.[24,29]

- Place your cell phone on airplane mode; do not open email, nor access social media.
  - Record what you have accomplished by using this technique throughout the week.
  - Is there a sense of increased control?
- Prohibit phone use during meals, then
  - assess the difference in the quality of family interaction.
  - note reduction in disruptions.

Partners should explore ways to be efficient with their time. It is easy to postpone a time-consuming commitment in favor of addressing less important activities that can be completed quickly. This behavior impedes progress on important tasks. To manage complex tasks, adopt a *divide and conquer* approach by splitting the project into manageable tasks. Completing each individual task ensures the project will eventually be completed. A reward when a task is completed such as a five-minute walk, a coffee break, or phoning a friend can reinforce the success.

Recognizing when a task is overwhelming and negotiating adjustments is more productive than turning to easier tasks. Ask for assistance when necessary and delegate when possible. Acknowledge unnecessary busy work and reallocate time productively.[24] "Technology is a good servant, but a bad master."[15]

Acknowledge that personal time is as much of a priority as work time. Today's available technology makes it far too easy to take work home or on vacation.[15,16,24,29] Unplug from work and turn off distractions that interfere with the time allocated for personal life, family, and friends. A partnership may afford significant flexibility, but it is the partners' responsibility to achieve a work-life balance.

Best practice for work-life balance is for partners to make deliberate choices about how to spend their time.[29] Choose at least one primary goal for the day and keep daily goals visible at all times. A simple *to do* list can reflect attainable goals, prioritizing the important tasks and putting nonessential ones into a *parking lot* to address when the high priority chores have been completed or a change of pace is needed.[16,29,24]

When evaluating volunteer service, consider depth versus breadth. For example, determine if devoting quality time to a single volunteer activity is more meaningful than investing short bursts of time and effort in several different endeavors. Each partner must determine how best to revive, refocus, revitalize, and savor those things that bring joy to life such as jogging, listening to music, or sitting on the back patio watching the sunset.[16,29,24,15]

Partners should consider family, friends, and one another when determining what is important, then develop a plan to meet their goals and maintain a quality work-life balance.[29] Partners should not assume others' responsibilities because they like things done their way. They must learn to accept another person's approach, leaving time to concentrate on what is important. Partners must communicate clearly and learn to say "no" in order to avoid overcommitment. Partners are human and subject to imperfection; they must do their best, then be okay with that.[24]

Managing Self

Achieving a higher level of wellness and well-being is an essential component of work/life balance. Imbalance can result in physical and psychological impairment, illness, obesity, and immobility, all of which can have a devastating personal and economic effect on the individual and the partnership. Incorporating periodic breaks into the work schedule promotes health and well-being. There are phone applications that remind one to stand up, to breathe, to clear the mind, and to refocus on the business at hand. Exercise can reduce stress, depression, and anxiety and can boost the immune system.[24] Partners should program a bit of fun and novelty into the daily schedule.

Participating meaningfully in an author partnership can represent a social connection between the partners as well as a business relationship.[16] Disharmony may occur when a spouse or life partner resents the time devoted to the partnership or the relationship that the author partners share. When a partnership functions within a traditional hierarchal work environment, such as several employees at different levels of employment collaborating to write a journal article, the collegial dynamics of a partnership may not be compatible with workplace dynamics.

Conflicting Obligations

Partners are rarely identical (equal) as each brings a different set of talents, strengths, and weaknesses to the partnership. Together they must arrange for the distribution of responsibilities and benefits to be balanced and fair (equitable). Equity is essential to the partnership as inequity breeds dissatisfaction and resentment,[31] and interferes with the partners' ability to achieve their goal. Partners maintain equity by accepting and discharging assignments compatible with their skills and working diligently together to achieve their goal.

Responsible partners address any perception of inequity and conflicting obligations immediately by setting aside time for discussion and negotiation. When one partner is oblivious to the needs of the other, the dissatisfied partner must speak up. At times, simply listening to one another's perceptions motivates the partners to explore alternatives and resolve the problem. Regular communication about what works and what does not work assists the partners in staying on track. Postponing discussion of critical issues and allowing challenges to slide can derail progress and doom the partnership. Recognizing avoidance behavior and promoting effective dialogue can prevent a major crisis.[29] Conversation early and often reinforces alignment and balance and allows work to advance in harmony.

When partners maintain a work-life balance, productivity increases. They experience fewer illnesses, and they are more likely to stay on task.[24] Partners must be honest and forthright with one another, maintaining sensitivity to one another's unique situation and point of view. For a solution to any problem to be effective, both partners must participate actively. In stressful times, they should step away and allow time to cool off before losing control so that they can deal with problems calmly, constructively, and effectively.[23]

The partners should seek to understand one another's boundaries and recognize how commitment to the partnership fits into their work and personal lives. Partners must trust and respect one another and communicate honestly; they must *say what they mean* and *mean what they say*. One of the most pressing challenges for partners may be to find the courage to speak up when one partner feels that the balance of work has become inequitable or the partnership agreement has been breached.[32] Partners must be flexible and assess equity over time. For instance, when one partner is on vacation, the other partner may continue working on the project. The work of the partnership may seem inequitable for short periods of time but should be balanced and fair over the course of the project.

Permitting commitment to the work of the partnership to overshadow commitment to family, friends, and personal health can result in damage to relationships that may be irreversible. Although the world does not end with a job loss or not getting an expected promotion or pay increase,[16] loss of health and family relationships cannot be as easily accommodated. For example, spending a bit less time on partnership activity is similar to being okay with a "little messiness" in the home such as dust on the furniture or the beds left unmade for a day in order to spend time with loved ones. Outsourcing cleaning or other tasks that take away from what is important, or restructuring the work of the partnership, may be important options to consider for maintaining balance.[15]

Conclusion

Successful partnering requires developing a strong sense of self, identifying personal values, and determining what is important in life. Establishing the meaning of work-life balance is unique to the individual and must be articulated among partners.[29] Partners who are self-aware know what success and happiness mean for them and know how to reward themselves when they attain their goals. At any point in time, a partner's focus may be skewed towards work or personal issues; however, balance is assessed by evaluating overall behavior. A partnership can bring joy and spontaneity when partners celebrate the milestones that represent progress toward their goal and recognize one another's special contributions in meaningful ways.

3

COMMITMENT

A partnership is essentially a *workplace without walls* with partners who are analogous to co-workers. The partners' promise obligates them to the partnership. This commitment is a crucial component of the success of a partnership. Meyer and Herscovitch described commitment as "a force that binds an individual to a course of action."[33] A carefully constructed action plan and a well-conceived infrastructure will not facilitate the success of a partnership unless the partners commit to fulfilling their obligations.

Types of Commitment

Commitment is a function of individual characteristics, one's relationship to the partnership, and other factors affecting the partner's ability to make decisions. Three types of commitment are addressed in this chapter: (a) *Personal Commitment* influenced by an individual's attitude, value, and affect; (b) *Continuance*

Commitment based on the partner's relationship with the partnership; and (c) *Normative Commitment* influenced by the partner's degree of obligation to remain with the partnership.

Personal Commitment

Personal (Value) Commitment, comprised of an individual's *attitude* and *behavior,* is a dominant model for assessing workplace commitment that can be applied to partnerships.[34] *Attitude* represents the partners' willingness to work based on their identification with the project goals and *behavior* represents what they are willing to do to achieve them. There is a reciprocal relationship between *attitude* and *behavior* and *personal commitment.*[35] The higher the partner's *personal* or *value commitment*, the more committed to the partnership goals (attitude) and more willing to exert the effort required to achieve them (behavior) the partner will be. The converse is also true. As commitment goes down, attitude and behavior suffer.

Meyer and Allen[36] contend that *personal commitment* - all of the feelings, both positive and negative, associated with participating in the partnership - is the first mindset that influences commitment. *Personal commitment* represents the partner's reasons for participating in or for leaving the partnership. The degree of *personal commitment* is determined by how important the partnership is to the partner. When partners' experiences are consistent with their expectations, *personal commitment* is strong or positive; conversely, a partner with a less satisfying experience would have a weak or negative *personal commitment.*

Continuance Commitment

Continuance commitment balances the partner's desire to stay in the partnership with how costly the partner perceives it will be to leave.[36,33] The partner who experiences *continuance commitment* may stay with the partnership to avoid giving up perceived fame and fortune, or because publishing is extremely important and would not be possible without participation in the partnership.

Normative Commitment

Normative commitment is the partners' perception of obligation to remain in the partnership, the perception that remaining is *the right thing to do*. The partner may feel obligated to the partnership for benefits received, such as paid conference registration, paid organization membership, or course attendance. *Personal, continuance,* and *normative commitment* represent the dominant model for assessing organizational and partnership commitment. Meyer and Allen[36] suggested that each type of commitment develops as the result of the partners' unique experiences that motivate their on-the-job behavior. Meyer and Allen's studies demonstrate that *personal commitment* is the strongest predictor of a partner's commitment to the partnership, but that commitment can be mitigated significantly by *normative* and *continuance commitment,* especially as personal commitment approaches ambivalence.[36]

3.1 On each scale below, indicate your level of commitment to the partnership with an **X** and record the rationale for your decision.

Figure 3.1: Commitment Scale

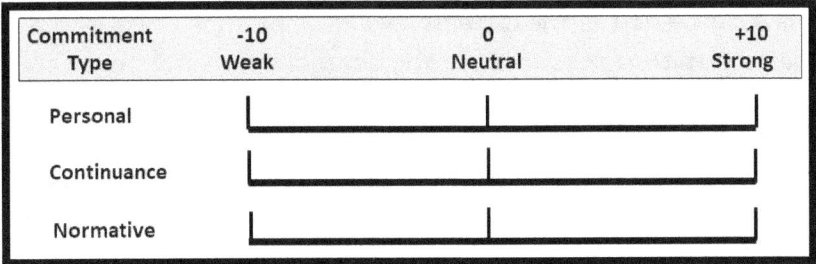

Influences on Commitment

While partnerships are formed for a variety of reasons, the commonality of partnering is the desire of two or more individuals to work together to achieve a goal that would be difficult for either to accomplish independently.[37] The success of the partnership depends upon each partner's commitment to the partnership goal (*attitude*) and the strength of each partner's willingness to invest the time, effort, and resources required *(behavior)*.[37]

Reeder[38] identifies four variables that influence commitment: (a) *treasures,* (b) *troubles,* (c) *contributions,* and (d) *choices*. *Treasures* represent the benefits that a partner associates with participation in the partnership. Some of the treasures will be shared by the partners; others will be unique and personal to an individual. The benefits perceived by each partner must be attractive enough to make it worth overcoming the *troubles,* challenges, and sacrifices partners face. At a minimum, the partners need to prioritize their personal resources and restructure their schedules to accommodate their commitment to the partnership.

Each partner must be willing and able to make four *contributions* to achieve the partnership's objectives: *time, money, expertise,* and *choice*.[38] *Time* and *money* are commodities that are often in short supply and the partners must plan carefully to incorporate the demands of the partnership into their schedules. Partnership success is dependent upon the partners' contribution of their diverse *expertise* - the unique blend of knowledge and skill that makes their participation valuable. The fourth variable, *choice,* is the most personal. Each partner must perceive that committing resources to the partnership is the best choice among the alternatives available.

Partnerships differ from traditional employment primarily in structure. Partners do not work *for* one another in a hierarchal relationship; they work *with* one another in a manner determined collaboratively. The care that partners take in structuring the partnership has a significant influence on the potential for achieving their objectives. The partners' commitment to the success of the partnership is reflected in their commitment to the vision, the structure, and the plan (*attitude*) and their willingness to do what it takes to achieve their goals (*behavior*).

Although the partners may have disparate reasons for joining a writing partnership, they must commit to mutual respect and productive negotiation. Each partner must participate actively in discussions to ensure that all decisions are collaborative. Situations on which partners do not agree become opportunities for discussion and negotiation where individual viewpoints, motivations, and needs are shared, alternatives are explored, and the partners' mutual respect ensures that decisions are mutual.

Statement of Commitment

The *Statement of Commitment* devised by the Global Humanitarian Project[39] identifies five promises that each partner must make in order to participate: (a) Equality/Equity, (b) Transparency, (c) Results-oriented focus, (d) Responsibility, and (e) Complementarity. By formally acknowledging commitment to the partnership, the partners demonstrate their understanding of the importance of each component and pledge to honor them.

Equality

The first promise, *equality/equity* of the partners, includes mutual respect and equitable distribution of obligations, responsibilities, and privileges based on resources, skills, and needs of the project. Although individual contributions by partners may vary widely depending upon the partnership structure and function, mutual respect is essential. Each partner's contribution is based on his/her unique skills and talents. Despite their contributions not being *equal,* the partners must perceive that their contributions are balanced and fair (*equitable*). Commitment wanes with the perception that one partner shoulders an unfair proportion of the burden.

The closer the alignment of the partnership goals with their individual perceptions of value, the more likely the partners are to perceive their participation as developmental, exciting, and fun. Partners who discuss their needs and expectations openly have a positive influence on the partnership's practices and culture.[18] When partners represent both genders, they must recognize the need for *gender equity* and avoid historical patriarchal relationships. Openly addressing prejudices, assumptions, and divergent ideas creates a culture that fosters success for everyone.[40] Overall, factors that can contribute to work-life conflict include hours worked, gender, the presence or absence of children, social class, age, domestic division of labor, and societal influences.[41]

Transparency

Transparency in the partnership refers to the partners' commitment to open communication and equal access to relevant information.[39] Partners are responsible for addressing their tasks with integrity and in a timely manner. Transparency promotes trust; the sharing of knowledge and resources facilitates productivity. The logistics of managing the partnership must include a mechanism for keeping all partners up-to-date on their individual and cumulative efforts. Tools such as calendars, worksheets, and task lists should be accessible to everyone, with each partner participating in keeping the data current.

Results-Oriented Focus

A *results-oriented focus* promotes activities and behaviors that are reality-based and action-oriented, that support both the interim and long-term goals of a project, and that respect the partners' individual strengths and weaknesses.[39] Clearly-defined responsibilities keep partners focused on moving the project forward. Regularly scheduled meetings support both transparency and productivity by reinforcing deadlines, providing progress updates, and establishing fixed targets for benchmarking progress. Regular updates facilitate revisions and course corrections that keep the project on track.

Responsibility

Partnerships differ in complexity, composition, and purpose. Most writing partnerships are part-time endeavors that must be incorporated into the partners' schedules along with their primary employment obligations and personal commitments. Partners' contributions must be measured over time. There will be instances when the workload may be unbalanced. For example, the partner responsible for managing the publishing process will be busiest at a different time from the partner responsible for the final edit of the manuscript. Partners have an ethical obligation to approach their tasks responsibly and with integrity, and to meet their obligations in a manner that is appropriate and relevant, committing to activities only when they have the means, competencies, skills, and capacity to complete their assignments.[39]

Complementarity

Complementarity refers to the concept that the partner's assets and contributions complement one another, creating relevance and balance among strengths and weaknesses.[39] As a team, the partners bring their combined skills to the project. Diversity among partners provides the opportunity to build upon strengths and compensate for weaknesses. Skills in management, accounting, and publicity are as important to the partnership as linguistic, artistic, and editing skills, but rarely does one partner excel in all of these areas. Any talent not provided by the partners themselves can be acquired by contracting with an outside individual or company.

Behaviors Consistent with Commitment

Hoque[42] proposed five behaviors essential to commitment: (a) *Be direct*, (b) *Think ahead*, (c) *Inspire and influence*, (d) *Create a community of support*, (e) *Think long term*. *Being direct* requires clarity of purpose and allows partners to stay focused on a common objective. Clear communication keeps progress consistent with the partnership's objectives. *Thinking ahead* facilitates continuity, prevents duplication of work, and allows the partners to prepare for situations that might interfere with productivity. For instance, acknowledging family obligations, vacations, and known upcoming events results in a realistic schedule for writing and publishing and prevent unnecessary delays and missed deadlines.

Competition for time and energy is not consistent because each partner has a unique personal life. Their attitudes toward one another influence their commitment to the partnership. They must commit to *inspire and influence* one another. Changes are inherent in a dynamic environment and *thinking long term* allows partners to anticipate the effect of future influences on partnership activities and investments. *Thinking long term* also ensures the continued relevancy of activities. In a rapidly changing world, a commitment to foresight and flexibility position the partnership to take advantage of new technology, fresh ideas, novel resources, and process improvements.[42] A plan of action may require frequent updates to remain on point and retain relevance.

Conclusion

The value that partners place on the goals of the partnership determines their willingness to devote the time, effort, and resources required to incorporate the partnership into their lives. Each partner brings a different combination of knowledge and skill to the writing project, and although their contributions may not be equal, each partner must consider the contributions equitable. Commitment implies respect for individual needs, support in times of challenge, and the willingness to contribute what is necessary to achieve partnership goals.

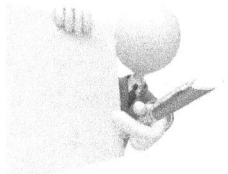

4

CONTRACT

Before beginning to write, the partners must explore and document their shared understanding of the project.[43,44] Critical elements for any partnership include openness and trust. Trust is the foundation for documenting the alignment (Chapter 1) of their expectations on all elements of the partnerships[45] and safeguarding the partners from disharmony, misunderstanding, and conflict.[46] The partners should favor documentation over an oral agreement. The partnership terms can be captured in minutes or policy; however, a well-written contract can prevent legal entanglements.[43] Publishers may also require partners to have a formal written agreement prior to engaging with them.[43]

The partners determine what their agreement or contract will include. Common aspects of author partnering that should be addressed are (a) ownership of copyright material should one partner leave the partnership for any reason, (b) author order, and (c) assignment of responsibilities for the business management of the partnership.

According to the *US Copyright Act, Section 101*[47], without any contract to indicate differently, the collective work of partners is considered to be owned equally and jointly by the authors.[48] In documenting their agreement, the partners are not bound by the Copyright Act section that requires that royalties be split equally among the owners of the copyright. They may choose to split in any ratio they prefer.

Once the contract is signed, it is legally enforceable and the partners' official relationship has begun.[49] Each partner should retain a copy of the signed contract. The value of flexibility becomes self-evident as the partners explore their relationship, develop their organizational structure and routines, and work to accommodate one another's needs. All decisions affecting the partnership and their work should be collaborative, with the contract serving as the primary resource when issues require resolution.[49]

We are not attorneys, and this chapter on contracts is not to be construed as legal advice. We respect the copyright law and firmly believe in the value of developing a written agreement between the partners. Partners should explore all contract elements together prior to signing the document.

Finding Sample Contracts

A variety of sample contracts is available online to download and customize for any partnership.

 **Contract Resources**

Sample Contracts:

- http://jamesaconrad.com/writing/author-collaboration.html[50]
- https://selfpubauthors.wordpress.com/2011/12/20/a-sample-co-author-contact/[51]

Additional Resources

- Recommendations related to forming a partnership[52]
  http://www.dmlp.org/legal-guide/forming-partnership
- 50-State Guide to Forming a Partnership[53]
  https://www.nolo.com/legal-encyclopedia/50-state-guide-establishing-general-partnership.html
- How to Make a Business a Partnership when a Partner Lives in Another State[54]
  https://info.legalzoom.com/make-business-partnership-partner-lives-another-state-22480.html
- Learn about the Specifics of a Partnership[55]
  https://www.thebalancesmb.com/what-should-be-included-in-a-partnership-agreement-398879

Elements of Agreement

Explore the various elements that each partner wishes to include in the contract. Discuss what the individual elements mean to each partner to ensure that your contract reflects your agreement.

4.1 Answering the following questions can assist in determining the elements of your contract.

- What is the purpose/goal of the partnership?
- How will each partner contribute to the goal?
- When will the work be completed?
- How will the product(s) be evaluated?
- How will a tie be broken?
- How will author order be established?
- Who will be the corresponding partner (communicate and negotiate with external team members)?
- What expenses will the partnership cover?
- Who will manage the partnership finances?
- How will proceeds be shared?
- What is the dissolution strategy?[44]

Each partner must be aware of the others' primary goals. For example, if recognition as an expert is important to one partner, then author order is significant. Another partner may place a higher value on royalties.[43] All contract elements must be in alignment with the partners' individual goals and expectations.

Success of the partnership depends upon developing a comprehensive business foundation.

Life events might prevent one partner from completing the project or from continuing at the same level of participation. Considering such possibilities early in the partnership, and making provisions in the contract for managing change can prevent confusion and discord. Negotiating the contract details can be an intense experience for the partners as the process forces them to step back and consider the implications of their decisions and to find shared meaning in their relationship in anticipation of a new and fulfilling interaction.[49]

Author Order and Roles

Determining author order before the project begins makes it easier to develop marketing materials early in the writing process. Partners can re-negotiate their decision should circumstances change. Identify the managing partner who will assume responsibility for the day-to-day management of the partnership: prepare meeting agendas, maintain minutes, manage shared programs and online platforms, and keep the partnership infrastructure intact.

Select the partner who will represent the partnership in communication with external team members. All partners should be copied on correspondence or receive a periodic summary report so that everyone is apprised of the business of the partnership. The corresponding author is the public face of the partnership and has a responsibility to ensure that correspondence reflects only those decisions in which all partners have participated.

In a partnership, one of the partners may have greater organizational and management skills while the other partner assumes primary responsibility for collating the contributions of all of the partners and editing the manuscript into a cohesive whole. However roles are apportioned among partners, all partners must participate in decision-making, and the contract should provide direction for managing situations when they cannot reach agreement.

Income and Expenses

If the partnership is an ongoing investment with the expectation of earning money from the sale of products, it should be set up as a small business which is inexpensive and relatively simple. Establish a *doing business as* name, open a bank account and consult a certified public account if necessary. An Employer Identification Number, a nine-digit number assigned by the Internal Revenue Service, is required for filing Federal and State taxes. For research studies and managing grant funding, the university or organization in which the partners are employed may provide these resources.

One partner should be responsible for managing the partnership finances including income and expenses, royalties, and tax returns. The partnership contract should identify what expenses the partnership will cover, what it will not, and how royalties will be disbursed. Managing the budget of a large research study may fall to one member of the partnership or the primary investigator when grants are involved.

Workload, Representation, and Warranties

The contract should identify the purpose of the partnership, detail the duties and responsibilities of the partners, and establish the expected delivery date of the project. Partners should explore the option of including an indemnity clause, or a promise to reimburse another party should the partnership work contain any false representation. For example, the partnership's products should not infringe on others' copyrights nor invade anyone's right to privacy. Declaration of these representations and warranties applies to all partners and guides decision making. The wording in contracts related to damages paid to others should address the potential for a breach of contract.[43]

To minimize liability, the partners should review their writing carefully for factual accuracy, particularly non-fiction and journal articles. In the US, *verifiable truth* is a defense to libel and partners should each "retain copies of all recorded interviews, transcripts, books, notes, letters and other research materials used in preparation of the work."[43] These documents can serve as the proof of permission to use specific content if a lawsuit for infringement of copyright were to emerge. Diligent record-keeping is imperative when using materials that are not the sole property of the partnership.[43]

The Copyright Permission and Libel Handbook: https://www.amazon.com/exec/obidos/ISBN=0471146544/copylawonlineA/[56]

Partner Disputes and Dissolution

Discussing contract elements early in partnership development when challenges can be prevented is more productive than waiting for a dispute to arise. Hypothetical scenarios can be discussed dispassionately. Protocols that the partners establish can be implemented objectively should an incident occur.[43] A well-conceived and well-written contract promotes clarity among partners and minimizes the potential for trust violations. Repairing a violated trust can be discouraging; however, the likelihood of repairing a breach depends on the *degree* to which the injured partner perceives the violation to be intentional.[46]

Confidentiality and non-compete clauses may be included in the contract to give direction should one partner want to separate from the partnership. Determine who will own any completed works of the partnership and any materials relating to projects in progress. Document how the funds in the accounts will be dispersed.

Lifshitz and Finkelstein[45] suggested there are two approaches to contract interpretation: textualist or *the letter of the law*, based on the literal meaning of the words, and contextualist or the *spirit of the law*, based on the consideration of additional information to determine the intended purpose of the wording. It is difficult to capture every eventuality that might surface in a contract; however, failure to address the interests of each partner can result in a contract that reflects neither the *letter* nor the *spirit* of the partners' initial intentions. The contract should be sufficiently comprehensive to reflect the expectations of the partners while providing the flexibility needed to address unforeseen circumstances. The contract development stage allows the partners to use their own creativity and innovation to make sure they have captured what both want. For partnerships, a context-dependent contract model where the interpretation is based primarily on the nature of the partners' relationship is appropriate.[45]

External Team Contracts

Partners may enter into contracts with freelance designers, editors, agents, publishers, etc. Sedwick[57] suggested that whether the partners are pursuing traditional publishing or self-publishing, they should review the elements in each contract carefully before signing it. Unfortunately, not all business entities are author-friendly or honest and fair. Partners should base affiliation decisions upon research, recommendation, and careful vetting. It is the partners' responsibility to ensure that any contract they sign clearly documents the purpose of the relationship, important elements of the relationship, and provisions that protect the partnership interests.

Check out Sedwick's[57] book: *Self-publisher's legal handbook: The step-by-step guide to the legal issues of self-publishing.* This book defines relevant legal terms and provides tables of elements for reflection during contract development.[57]

Conclusion

Selecting the partnership elements upon which decisions should be made can be a learning process that promotes the partners' alignment. The process should begin early in partnership development and the partners should reach an agreement prior to beginning the writing project. Documenting the partners' expectations and commitments can prevent hurt feelings, loss of money, and irreparable rifts in the relationship by providing guidelines for resolving disagreement. Agreement among partners should be clearly articulated in the contract, or recorded in minutes or policy. In any case, the agreement must be a clear reflection of the decisions and expectations of the partners on each of the critical elements of the partnership.

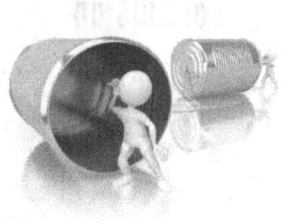

5

COMMUNICATION

Of all of the Cs, *communication* has the greatest influence on the success of a partnership. Through the use of language, conversation styles, non-verbal messages, and written communications, partners convey their ideas, thoughts, and feelings. The most innovative ideas, the best structure, the most sophisticated process will produce disappointing results in the absence of effective communication.

Simply delivering information is only part of the communication process.[58] How information is received is influenced by both verbal and non-verbal behaviors. Cooper-Duffy and Eaker[59] contend that communication skills include rapport-building to facilitate mutual respect and responsive listening that enables partners to acknowledge both the content and the emotional context of a message.

Effective communication implies the ability to reach decisions with constructive consensus. Communication within a partnership requires an environment that encourages questioning, investigating, persuading, negotiating, explaining, motivating, and delegating.[60] A carefully built infrastructure ensures that information is timely, shared, and retrievable.

Communication Styles

Recognizing and accommodating diverse communication styles strengthens relationships among partners, promotes engagement, and enhances the viability of a partnership.[61] Effective communication requires that each partner understand how the other partners process information. They must also be willing to negotiate and collaborate when their views differ. Knowing a partner's communication style can lead to purposeful discourse that is both understood and well-received.

DISC® profiles, based on the work of psychologist William Moulton Marston,[62] describe four personality types: *Dominant*, *Influencer*, *Steady*, and *Conscientious*. Each type is associated with a primary communication style that can provide a basis for targeting communication effectively among partners. All individuals have traits in more than one quadrant; however, everyone has a primary communication style.

Dominant partners are action-oriented, appreciate challenge, and focus on results.[62] They are big picture thinkers and tend to leave the details to their *Conscientious* colleagues, the analyzers and thinkers who value precision and competency. *Dominant* partners don't ramble or waste time. They respond best to communication that is organized and to the point, with facts presented logically and efficiently. *Dominants* appreciate being given alternatives and choices so that they can decide how to move forward.

Conscientious colleagues are careful, cautious, accurate and tactful. They prefer more formal communication with facts and data to support a position.[62] They appreciate hearing all sides of an issue and need time to analyze material before deciding. They respond best when there is clarity around expectations and deadlines.[62]

Influencers are social, warm, enthusiastic, and trusting[63] and thrive on relationships. They are good collaborators but may become side-tracked and lose focus. Ensure their active engagement in conversation by acknowledging their ideas and goals and providing data to support alternatives. *Influencers* may be motivated by testimonials from people they respect. They appreciate clear direction with details in writing, and they are prone to leaving decisions up in the air.[62]

The *Steady* individual is calm, patient, consistent, and values stability, loyalty, and personal relationships.[63] *Steadies* respond best when they are not rushed into making decisions. They appreciate when others listen carefully, ask specific questions, and demonstrate sensitivity to their feelings.

Partners must recognize that their leadership styles may vary. Each leadership type has its own communication style, work habits, and approach to setting priorities. There is less confusion and misinterpretation when partners understand and respect the diversity among them. Partners who can tailor their communication to optimize understanding and take advantage of the strengths of other partners' styles will be the most effective.

Purposeful Communication

Purposeful communication requires the sensitivity and foresight to craft a clear and concise message that creates a connection between the written word and the receiver. An effective communicator strives to promote a positive relationship with others and respects their unique methods of processing information.[64] Both speaker and writer must be sensitive to the information others consider valuable.

Readers will discard an article or book and listeners will *tune out* if they think they already know what is being said. Communicators must acknowledge what their target already knows, and begin with what they want and need. This demonstration of empathy and respect for the receiver will capture their attention and earn their trust.

5.1 Suggestions for improving communication (5.1.a) in the partnership, (5.1.b) with external team members and with readers include:

- Determine what they know and what they need to know.
- Assess communication for strengths and weaknesses.
- Identify their concerns and needs.
- Choose the most appropriate communication style.
- Be clear and concise; get to the point; keep it simple.
- Be truthful; build credibility.
- Include facts, examples, or stories for clarification.[64]

Words convey a message, but context is carried in non-verbal cues. Without tone, posture, gestures, or facial expressions, there can be a lack of depth in communication. "It's Friday" is a statement of fact, but the words do not indicate whether the speaker is excited about a weekend adventure or dejected at the thought of having to work all weekend. Emoticons, common in electronic communication, represent non-verbal cues and mimic those in live conversations. The same example used previously, "It's Friday," accompanied by a smiley-face emoticon produces a clearer message.

Positive communication, when it is recognized as heartfelt and genuine, has a greater effect than negative in stimulating motivation and productivity. Engaged and enthusiastic behaviors provide a constructive foundation for partners. Boundaries are sometimes created through negative tone, frustration, or disappointment. Keeping communication focused on the issue, not the individual, helps the partners maintain a constructive environment. Using positive and open gestures encourages open discussion and conversation. Positive tone, sustained eye contact, and open facial expressions communicate active listening and engagement.[65] When giving direction, address what the individual is supposed to do, reserving what not to do for preventing critical errors.

The timing of communication is also important. Allow people ample time to do what they need to do with the information provided. For instance, send notice of a meeting in plenty of time for attendees to prepare adequately. Then, a meeting reminder sent closer to the meeting date will ensure that attendees have not forgotten and will allow time for last minute preparations.

Communication Tools

Choose communication tools that are appropriate for both the message and the recipient. Communication tools may include websites for ready access to both historical and current information, email and messaging programs for rapid communication, and social media sites for personal engagement. A phone call is an appropriate vehicle for both a message of some urgency and the need to make a personal connection.

Email is a rapid and convenient method of sharing information with one or more individuals at the same time. Recipients can choose to address emails *only* when time permits. Sorting through messages is time-consuming, and sometimes an email must be opened and reviewed to determine whether the information is valuable. Email etiquette suggests a relevant subject line and enough information in the first couple of sentences to give the recipient a good idea of what to expect.

When replying to an email, be respectful of people's time by determining if the reply should be sent to all of the recipients or just to the sender.[66] The body of an email is appropriate for short messages. Put long messages in a document and send as an attachment. If clarity is an issue, follow up with a phone call or a meeting.

Text messaging is appropriate for short messages. Even when recipients are busy, they can glance at the message to determine its importance and respond immediately or wait to reply at a suitable time. Reserve text messages for timely information such as updates that are important to the recipient. Consider turning off messaging when focusing on a task to prevent distraction that interferes with progress toward an objective.[67]

Listening: A Means of Communication

Active listening, sometimes called empathic or reflective listening, implies fully concentrating on what is being said. Listening applies to both the spoken and written word. People use their senses and non-verbal cues to understand the speaker's or author's message and associated emotions and perspectives.[68] The speaker's expressions, posture, gestures, and tone enhance the verbal message for active listeners who give the speaker their undivided attention. Sentence structure, tone, timeliness, and images help a reader interpret a writer's emotions and perspective.

Active listening improves mutual understanding.[69] **L-I-S-T-E-N** and **S-I-L-E-N-T** are anagrams; the word pair reminds us that it is essential to be quiet and pay attention.[70] Active listening also implies internal silence. Listen without judging the message, without preparing a response, and without waiting impatiently for the opportunity to jump into the conversation.

Active listeners also demonstrate their undivided attention with posture and body language. They lean forward and encourage the speaker through eye contact, a smile, or a nod. They do not interrupt, but wait for the speaker to pause before asking questions or giving feedback. They reflect on the speaker's message, validate their perceptions, and explore the implications of the message before responding with ideas of their own. (Figure

5.1). In a partnership, effective listening contributes to making fewer errors and wasting less time. Effective listening empowers partners to make meaningful decisions and build friendships.[71]

Figure 5.1: Ten Steps to Effective Listening[71]

10 Steps to Effective Listening
1. Face the speaker and maintain eye contact.
2. Be attentive, but relaxed; mentally screen out distractions.
3. Keep an open mind; listen without judging or jumping to conclusions.
4. Listen to the words and try to picture what the speaker is saying; build a mental model.
5. Don't interrupt and don't impose your "solutions."
6. Wait for the speaker to pause before asking clarifying questions.
7. Ask questions only to further understanding. Don't derail a conversation by changing the subject.
8. Try to feel what the speaker is feeling.
9. Give the speaker regular feedback. Show that you understand the speaker's perspective.
10. Pay attention to what *isn't* said and to non-verbal cues.
11. Bonus: Conclude with a summary statement[71]

Partnerships profit from diversity of thought when partners seek to learn from one another. With the give and take of dynamic communication, all partners develop a stake in the decisions they make. Listening actively facilitates an environment where the final decisions are enhanced versions of the initial positions of the partners. Synergistic outcomes that are greater than the sum of the parts promote increased buy-in. Diversity of thought guards against groupthink and overconfidence[72] and promotes the idea that the culture, background, and experiences of each individual are unique and needed.[73]

Bridging the Generation Gap

Diversity in perspective and practice enriches a partnership culture when the strengths and values of partners representing different generations are valued and incorporated.[74] At the same time, the partners must recognize, embrace, and overcome the communication challenges that accompany diversity.

Differences among the generations stem from the disparate cultures in which each cohort was raised and the communication resources available at the time. Boomers (born 1945-1965) and Generation Xer's (born 1965-1980) were encouraged to be more independent than Millennials (born 1980-2000), who were often raised by helicopter parents intimately involved in their children's lives.[75] Boomers were born when television was the predominant source of communication; Generation Xer's grew up during the computer revolution, and Millennials have never known a world without mobile technology.[76] Although congruent values among partners and balance between work and leisure are important concepts in a partnership, they may be interpreted differently among the generations.[77]

Boomers have been called the "show me" generation.[78] They are serious, focused, and generally favor "live" communication with face-to-face meetings, telephone conversations, and printed documents. They have come to recognize the efficiency of email for sharing information that does not require significant interpretation, but they may prefer a phone conversation to back-and-forth emails.[78] Generation Xer's are highly educated with high job expectations and a strong commitment to work-life balance. They are pragmatic, technologically literate, and big-picture thinkers.

Millennials' approach to communication is instant, playful, collaborative, expressive, responsive, and flexible.[79] They like immediate communication, virtual documents, and social media. Boomers who *live to work* and the younger generations who *work to live* must collaborate to discover a balance between the authentic and engaging challenges in their personal and work lives.[77] Partners must be willing to address their divergent opinions with candor.[80] Recognizing that diversity of thought and style enrich the partnership enhances partners' commitment to one another and to the partnership goals.[81] Focusing on the value that diversity brings to problem-solving often facilitates a solution that is more effective than any of the original recommendations.

Diversity in Communication

Preference for communication tools varies among individuals and age groups. There is rarely a single right way to communicate. The unique combination of content and audience in any given situation provides an opportunity to tailor communication for maximum effectiveness. For instance, a face-to-face meeting may be broadcast so that those unable to attend in person can participate, and content may be captured electronically for those unavailable at the time of the meeting. Sending a combination of meeting reminders by email, text, and postcard is another example of respecting disparate communication preferences.

Advances in technology occur so rapidly that devices that existed 50 years ago are now obsolete.[82] It may be difficult for different generations to appreciate and adapt to communication styles other than their own.[83] Millennials and Generation Xer's tend to embrace digital, interactive technologies; Boomers may be slow to adapt to them. Boomers are using email, *Facebook®, Twitter®,* and *LinkedIn®*; Millennials have moved on to instant communication like texting, *Instagram®* and *Snapchat®*. They may also use graphics and Internet slang instead of complete sentences, often sharing just an image or photo with no text.

Infrastructure

Efficiency in achieving partnership objectives requires a well-designed infrastructure comprised of tools that both facilitate the work of the partnership and respect the communication styles and needs of the partners. Making appropriate product and protocol decisions should be done collaboratively among partners to ensure that everyone's needs and preferences are considered.

Management Tools

Writing partnerships may determine that a virtual office system is more cost-effective and efficient than a brick and mortar location. Current technology provides a wide variety of tools to meet business needs and keep the partners connected. A myriad of online programs for managing, sharing, and storing work products such as *Google Drive®* or *DropBox®* afford the partners the flexibility to work and collaborate at any time, particularly when they are geographically distant from one another. Each partner's edits can be color-coded to facilitate communication and the negotiation inherent in the development of a jointly-written manuscript.

An updated online calendar such as *Google Calendar®* or *Outlook®* keeps the partnership schedule accessible at all times. Cloud-synced document storage provides partners with the ability to work on shared documents and to access the most current version of a document at any time.[84] Project management tools like *Slack®*, *Kanbanflow®*, and *Trello®* help partners keep projects organized and up to date.

A monthly, weekly, or daily backup system, depending upon the frequency of revisions, is essential for ensuring the safety of electronic documents. Maintaining copies of partnership documents in more than one location ensures that the failure of one computer system will not jeopardize the viability of the partners' work.

Meetings

In-person meetings, either face-to-face or virtual video conferencing, promote interaction among partners, update the pool of shared knowledge, and keep partners current. Meetings also contribute to the *social mind* of a partnership, a dynamic and creative force that promotes better ideas, plans, and decisions.[85] For those partners who are able, meeting on a regular basis can ensure consistent communication and collaboration. Using an agenda supports the meeting by making good use of the partners' time. A well-constructed meeting process can foster creativity, enhance energy level, and encourage synergistic activities for the partners to get their work accomplished.

A routine meeting can be managed efficiently on an online meeting platform like *Skype®*, *Zoom®*, or *Bluejeans*™. With a web camera and microphone, partners can see and hear one another, share their computer screens, and work on documents together. Keeping the agenda visible throughout the meeting facilitates progress and ensures that all items are addressed. Digital meeting platforms save both time and money since travel is unnecessary and the platforms, with basic features, are available at limited to no cost.

Meetings facilitate accountability, motivate partners to complete assignments in a timely fashion, and provide an opportunity for partners to enjoy their social connection. In small partnerships, meetings are often casual; however, the meeting location, whether face-to-face or online, must be free of distractions and have the resources necessary to implement the meeting agenda. Unless a private room is available, a restaurant or coffee shop is not the best meeting venue.

Strategic planning and problem-solving are best done live or synchronously where facial expressions, tone, and body language that comprise up to 93% of communication can provide important clues to the partners' positions.[86] The energy created with live discussion increases focus and enhances creativity. Periodic live meetings help to reinforce partners' commitment to the partnership and to one another.

Meetings must be purposeful, compelling, and focused on providing information and resolving outstanding issues.[87] Regularly scheduled meetings should be postponed when there is nothing new on the agenda. Comprehensive minutes or an annotated agenda document the status of ongoing activities and lend continuity to meetings by reflecting accomplishments, outstanding assignments, deadlines, and next steps. Providing the agenda at least 24 hours in advance of the meeting encourages partners to prepare and allows for last-minute input. The partners can decide how to manage responsibility for maintaining the agenda (Figure 5.2) and recording minutes.

Figure 5.2: Sample Agenda

PARTNERSHIP NAME
(Mission/Vision Statement)
AGENDA

DATE:
LOCATION:
TIME:

Review of Minutes:

Continuing Business:

New Business:

Next Steps & Assignments:

Next Meeting Date/Time/Location:

Parking Lot:

Project management tools such as *Kanbanflow®* or *Trello®* are designed to highlight a project's key elements and track progress toward completion. The partners identify each of the project components and list the activities required to complete it, then organize the components into categories and establish timelines. Each partner updates the tool to reflect progress on any project component by checking off completed activities and moving the component from one category or time frame to another.

Conclusion

Written and verbal skills are essential. Communication involves questioning, investigating, persuading, negotiating, explaining, motivating, and delegating. Rather than a *one size fits all* phenomenon, communication must be tailored to the speaking and listening styles of the participants.

Listening is an integral component of communication. More than just hearing the speaker's words, listening involves observation and using one's senses to understand the speaker's emotions and position. A partnership must construct a communication platform including email, an online meeting program, and cloud storage so the partners can meet, work individually and together, and manage the business of their partnership. The partners should make platform decisions collaboratively.

Purposeful communication sends a clear, concise, and meaningful message. Age, culture, and communication style may differ among partners, so tailoring communication appropriately is essential to promote harmony and facilitate understanding of the partners' disparate positions on issues, recommendations, and expectations.

6

CONFLICT RESOLUTION

When individuals with different personalities, leadership styles, and skill sets work together, conflict is inevitable. The distinction between constructive and destructive conflict lies in the way the partners handle it.[88] They can avoid crises by addressing conflict during the alignment (Chapter 1) phase of the partnership. Through open discussion of strengths and weaknesses, partners can adopt conflict resolution strategies before the emotions inherent in facing an actual conflict can interfere. When partners combine analysis of a conflict with critical thinking, they can discover a rich array of alternative considerations.[89]

Conflict resolution strategies and protocols are generally consistent with the partners' leadership styles and expectations and are reflective of the partnership's culture, norms, beliefs, and values.[90] Conflicts vary in intensity and in their potential to affect productivity, so a single conflict resolution strategy may not be appropriate for every situation.

Conflict can be a catalyst for creativity or it can lead to a nexus of competing agendas, divisiveness, and hostility that diminishes trust and halts productivity.[91] Resolving conflict can be productive when partners recognize that disparities in their backgrounds, experiences, and perceptions can become opportunities for growth and innovation, cohesion and trust. Proactive conflict resolution can promote effective personal and partnership performance and a sharpened sense of identity and solidarity.[92]

Resolving Conflict by Leadership Style

According to Graham,[93] almost everything written about conflict management today is reflective of Follett's seminal work on *Constructive Conflict*. Follett[94] recognized conflicts as a natural and inevitable part of life that do not lead to negative outcomes if addressed with an analytical and imaginative mindset. Follett proposed three tactics for resolving conflict: *domination, compromise,* and *integration*. Blake and Mouton[95] expanded Follett's work into five leadership styles: (a) Impoverished, (b) Country Club, (c) Middle of the Road, (d) Task Oriented, and (e) Team Management, then described the approach to conflict resolution associated with each style. See Figure 6.1 for a matrix identifying the relative concern for *people* and *productivity* for each leadership style and approach to managing conflict.[95]

Figure 6.1 Leadership Styles and Conflict Resolution Strategy[95]

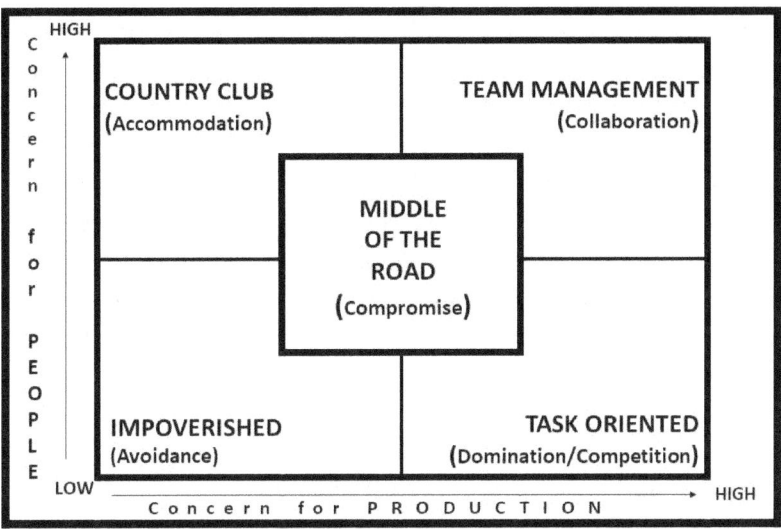

Developed from Blake and Mouton's content.[95]

Conflict resolution strategies are consistent among individuals within each style of leadership.[95] Follett's[94] *domination* strategy is associated with the Task-Oriented leader; *compromise* with the Middle of the Road leader; *integration* associates in varying levels with the three remaining styles. The relationship between winning and losing differentiates the styles from one another. The Team Management leader favors a win/win approach while the Task Oriented leader favors win/lose. A Middle of Road leader favors a vote where majority wins. If one partner grudgingly concedes to the majority, the result is capitulation, not integration.[94,95]

Impoverished Leader and Avoidance Strategy

The impoverished partner is a laissez-faire leader with minimal commitment to the other partners or to productivity.[95] Avoidance is rarely an appropriate strategy for conflict resolution since there is no opportunity for the participants to express themselves or to explore an outcome acceptable to either party. Consistently avoiding conflict diminishes the productivity of the partnership. Partners become resentful when they perceive that their thoughts, ideas, and needs are marginalized, reducing their dedication to the partnership and diminishing their productivity.[95]

Although this leadership style does not seem impressive, the partnership might accept such a partner if he/she brings specific knowledge or skills such as writing, editing, illustrating, or contacts in the industry that help the partnership achieve its objectives. The impoverished leader avoids conflict, maintaining neutrality by making him/herself unavailable to deal with any situation that requires conflict resolution.[95]

Country Club Leader and Accommodation Strategy

The Country Club partner is focused on maintaining a neutral environment[95] and promoting peaceful coexistence among the partners. This partner strives to maintain harmony by accommodating, smoothing over, or ignoring discord. Accommodation can be an appropriate approach for low stakes conflicts that have little potential for interfering with partnership dynamics or productivity.[95]

As long as accommodation is a shared experience and the instances of each partner's accepting the other's position are equivalent, there should be no residual hard feelings or harboring of grudges. Healthy accommodation represents the normal give and take among partners who acknowledge one another's different strengths and skills, as long as decisions are more frequently based on objectivity than emotion.[95]

Task-Oriented Leader and Domination/Competition Strategies

Domination strategy describes the triumph of one party over the other (win/lose).[93] The Task-Oriented leader or the produce-or-perish partner is focused primarily on productivity and is supportive only of those who enhance production. Partners with this leadership style suppress conflict with an authority-obedience approach that can lead to a win-lose power struggle.[95] Partners with a more moderate approach to conflict resolution might have to step into a situation involving this type of leader in order to model a positive approach to resolving discord that is better for the partnership. Although domination sounds like an unacceptable situation, it can be an efficient approach for minor disagreements where the loser can accept the resolution without feeling defeated. Conflicts over purchasing options or meeting venues and situations that involve an either/or decision can often be resolved successfully in this manner.

Competition as a conflict resolution strategy, *my way or the highway,* can only be effective when the partnership is neither productive nor running smoothly and there is disagreement among partners. The period can be fraught with tension and discord, and the competition is resolved only when one partner or faction prevails. If the loser chooses to subordinate his/her position to the winner, the partnership can move forward. If the loser remains with the partnership but does not truly accept the winner's decision, the continuing tension will undermine the stability of the partnership.

Middle of the Road Leader and Compromise Strategy

Integration requires debate, the exploration of alternatives, and the crafting of a resolution that appeals to all partners. Compromise, favored by Middle of the Road leaders,[95] is the most common conflict resolution tactic, but not the best approach for all situations. Compromise is considered extreme-aversion, the pursuit of the middle or safe ground on which participants can agree. It is a strategy best suited to situations with minor implications for the health of the partnership. A middle ground is achieved through bargaining where everyone involved gives and gets a little so that everyone wins (and loses) something.[93]

Based upon the resolution, compromise can be interpreted as *win/win, lose/lose,* or *win/lose* depending upon each partner's interpretation of how much he or she had to give up.[96,97] The compromise can be perceived as a sacrifice, and determining whether the sacrifice is worth it or not depends on the degree of commitment the partner has to the partnership and to each of the partners.[98]

Proponents of compromise consider it a win-win strategy because both sides participate in the negotiation and are presumed to be satisfied with the final decision. Detractors of compromise claim it creates a *lose/lose* situation because each party must give up something that was initially important.[93] Compromise is an appropriate conflict strategy when all of the partners believe that the resolution was fair and equitable. A compromise is not a good solution when one partner walks away feeling like a loser.

Stephen Covey[99] identified five explicit elements involved in a win-win agreement:

- Desired results (not methods) identify what is to be done and when.

- Guidelines specify the parameters (principles, policies, etc.) within which results are to be accomplished.

- Resources identify the human, financial, technical, or organizational support available to help accomplish the results.

- Accountability sets up the standards of performance and the time of evaluation.

- Consequences specify – good and bad, natural and logical – what does and will happen as a result of the evaluation.[99]

Team Management and Collaboration Strategy

The most robust conflict resolution strategy is *collaboration,* a purposeful activity that requires the greatest investment of time and effort of all of the approaches.[100,101] Collaboration is appropriate when the partners perceive that the conflict can have a significant effect on the future of the partnership. Strong leaders tend toward fixing problems through constructive confrontation and crucial conversations[102] focused on identifying the source of the problem and seeking a creative resolution.[103] Collaboration involves considering the partners' various points of view objectively, then weighing them against facts, emotions, reservations, and doubts.

Collaboration is an exploration strategy with the goal of considering all options in crafting the resolution that best supports the partnership objectives. Use of collaboration strategies creates a problem-solving environment where the partners evaluate alternatives and consider the facts. Through collaboration and productive dialogue, partners can produce a more creative and robust resolution than any of the original alternatives.[104] Collaboration can be successful only when those involved aligned on the partnership's core values are fully assertive and cooperative, and are willing to explore alternatives without bias.

A willingness to seek integrative solutions is essential to the development of a collaborative environment. Collaboration requires the partners to consider the issue from one another's perspective, to be objective and unbiased, and to avoid making assumptions. The partners must explore the contributing factors and seek creative solutions. They must engage in a balanced interchange of ideas and perceptions, clear and authentic communication, and purposeful listening. Collaborating builds strong relationships and strengthens the fabric of the partnership.

Although collaboration is the most socially acceptable approach[105] and has the highest potential for identifying a solid solution for meeting partnership needs, it is not appropriate for resolving all conflicts. Collaboration requires objectivity and maturity and time for the partners to pay careful attention to the process. Collaboration should be reserved for conflicts that have the greatest influence on the success of the partnership.

6.1 Record your preferred and secondary styles of conflict resolution on Figure 6.1 independently, then discuss with one another.

Conclusion

The key to choosing a conflict resolution strategy is an accurate determination of the potential impact of the conflict on the partners' relationship and the partnership's productivity.[106] The conflict resolution approach that has the potential for facilitating the most robust outcomes is collaboration, a process based on considering all options and devising a solution that is better than any of the initial alternatives. Less detailed approaches to conflict resolution such as compromise, accommodation, or domination may be appropriate for conflicts that have less impact on the overall process and goals of the partnership. Conflict, handled purposefully and appropriately, with careful analysis and critical thinking, can be a catalyst for innovation and improvement.

7

COMMERCE

The term *commerce* relates to *marketing strategies* that generate sales. For authors, it means moving books and articles from concept to the reader. Simply put, it is the process of putting the right product in the right place for the right price and at the right time.[107] Writing partnerships are often small to medium-size enterprises (SME) whose partners may have little experience with managing a business and often identify sales and marketing among the biggest challenges they face.[108]

Marketing protocols were initially developed for large corporations, but they are also relevant to SMEs. Partners are highly motivated because they are in control of their own destiny. They are usually risk-takers, excel at networking, and developing contacts as a means of promoting their product. They must be action-oriented, flexible, and creative and should address their marketing strategy when they first begin to write.

This chapter contains introductory information on developing the partnership's marketing plan using the Marketing 4Ps (product, place, promotion, and price) and the role of online communication systems for disseminating information efficiently and effectively. At a minimum, the authors' marketing platform should include a website, an email distribution program, and a social media presence.

The 4Ps: Marketing Mix

The *marketing mix* is a dynamic combination of policies and procedures that create a flexible platform adaptable to a variety of products and readers.[109] McCarthy[110] distilled the *marketing mix* into the 4Ps (product, price, place, promotion), a rubric used globally to highlight characteristics that differentiate one product or service from another. The 4Ps represents the elements of marketing that partners can control to ensure their product has maximum appeal.[111] The *marketing mix* is a fit with the competitive strategies in emerging markets and the nature of the competitive free market environment, demonstrated by performance outcomes for those authors who use the model. Authors focus the 4Ps on the target readers, addressing them in concert, not sequentially.

Over the years, in direct response to crucial changes in readers, service, e-commerce, and social media, additional Ps have been suggested. These include people, process, physical environment, partnerships, public, publicity, promotions, and profits. Although these elements are important, they represent content that can be incorporated in one of the original 4Ps.[112] The marketing process includes face-to-face communication, a website, electronic communication with a target market, and online platforms that support communication among individuals or that reach large numbers of people simultaneously.

Product

Product relates to the traits and functionality that distinguish the authors' item from others that are similar, or the product's *unique brand*. The brand incorporates the partnership name, series title, and packaging, etc. Product is about consumer wants and needs. Marketing begins with the concept of the product and its characteristics (e.g., genre, design, characters, features, packaging) that differentiates it from its competition and establishes its unique position in the marketplace. Lauterborn[113] asserted that readers have become sophisticated purchasers since the post-WW II purchasing frenzy and buy only what they want to buy.

Mass media has altered the environment in which products are sold, increasing both product consumption and access to readers.[113] Emphasis on product development, features, and differentiation from similar products continues to increase with the rapid expansion of competition in the marketplace and the ease of online searching for comparison products. Acceptability of a product is determined by its ability to meet or exceed readers' needs.[114,115] For authors of both fiction and non-fiction, investigating the competition is essential to designing the best product and determining the features that will differentiate it from the competition. In order to attract readers, a new contribution must provide product information, unique perceptions, new insights, or a novel storyline with interesting plot twists.

Place

Place refers to product accessibility, potential customers or target readers, and the locations where they will search for the product. Accessibility, based on product availability and convenience, defines the customers' ability to acquire and use the product.[113] With the proliferation of online marketing, convenience[113] has become significant because purchasing items from a brick and mortar establishment is now only one of the options available to readers. The percentage of electronic books sales more than doubled from 2013 to 2018.[116] Accessibility of the product on the Internet has become more important than where it can be found in the physical world.[117] Authors must identify appropriate journals for articles or locate distributors, wholesalers, and retailers for books.

Authors need to identify their target readers, including what, how, and where they prefer to buy. Investigating options for showcasing the product depends upon learning what similar products are selling in the marketplace and where the target readers encounter the products they purchase. The goal is to make the product easily accessible. Consumers today enjoy the convenience of a phone, online catalogs, and electronic payment transactions. Wider distribution channels provide competition for the few remaining landmark stores in each purchasing category.[113]

Publishing options for fiction and non-fiction products include either self-publishing (indie) or the traditional method that involves soliciting an agent and publisher. Among the reasons for the rise in popularity of indie publishing are the author's ability to maintain total creative control of the content, the shortened time span from completion of the manuscript to published product, flexibility with pricing and distribution,[118] and the emphasis that traditional publishers now place on the author's active participation in marketing their work.

Promotion

Promotion includes advertising, publicity, sales support, and public relations efforts to introduce the product to the target readers. Authors must develop sales strategies for getting the product into the hands of readers.[109] Promotion involves product knowledge and brand awareness, the relationship of their work to similar products in the marketplace.[114,115] For example, all romance novels follow a standard format; therefore, an author writing romance must follow that standard while providing something unique to capture the interest of romance readers. Promotion strategies should focus on the unique elements of the partners' work that differentiate it from competitive products.

Advertising typically refers to paid radio and television commercials, print ads, and Internet exposure. Public relations efforts refer to exhibits, events, conferences, press releases, infomercials, and sponsorship opportunities. Additional opportunities for exposure are created through personal connections and the direct involvement of the partners. Satisfied readers are the authors' most convincing tool for impressing other potential readers; reviews and recommendations are an excellent source of product promotion.

Purchasing decisions are intensely data-driven. With the proliferation of Internet marketing (eCommerce), *word of mouth* has transitioned to *word of mouse*.[108] Authors encourage satisfied readers to leave a comment or review on the partners' website, on websites like *Goodreads®* where readers provide recommendations[119], on *Amazon®* or *Book Nook®*, or wherever they purchased the book. When the price is higher, readers seek information to mitigate the risk of investing in a first-time purchase. As many as 95% of online shoppers (n=122,000) read reviews before making a purchase; providing reviews can more than double sales.[120]

Price

Price influences the marketing strategy and determines the potential for partnership profit. Affordability is determined by customers' willingness to pay a given price for a product or service.[115] Dollars represent only part of the cost of a purchase.[113] The term *cost to satisfy* includes the time and money spent searching, researching, decision-making and traveling to purchase the product.[113]

When a partnership is new to the market, it is unlikely that target readers will pay a higher price for their work than the competition. At the same time, pricing helps to shape the perception of a product. The goal is to divine the *sweet spot,* the price between too low (inferior product) and too high (not yet supported by evidence).[121]

7.1 Together, explore strategies for addressing the 4Ps of Marketing.

- Product
- Place
- Promotion
- Price

Online Systems

Authors must market their business, their products, and themselves in as many ways as possible to gain the attention of those who read electronically and those who use traditional sources like bookstores and libraries. Anwar and Daniel[122] noted the most frequently used entrepreneurial strategies included the development of a website, use of social media, and word-of-mouth marketing. These platforms should be addressed early in the development of the partnership infrastructure. It is human nature to communicate, socialize, recommend, comment, and alert one another to new content. Websites and social media are indispensable vehicles for communication and commerce.[123] A social platform enhances the potential for communicating with an ever-widening group of people by facilitating interaction with existing readers and fostering relationships with new followers.

Website and Blogs

The role of a website as a marketing tool for small business has grown steadily in recent years.[124] The authors' website is a showcase for the partnership to introduce books, house a blog, and manage and promote sales.[125] The site must be well-designed, kept up-to-date, and offer benefits for those who visit consistently to ensure that the authors develop a following that translates into sales.

Website appeal has three components: the ability to impress and capture attention, the extent to which readers perceive it to be pleasing, engaging, and appropriate, and whether it provides an opportunity for follow up and interaction.[126] The partnership's framework for website development must include resources for technology and marketing to ensure that it both engages readers and manages sales.

Readers formulate their first impressions quickly. The site must be visually appealing, well-organized, easily navigable, and contain engaging content. Reineke et. al.[127] maintained that visual complexity and color are the first considerations for website development because the aesthetic components are decisive in engaging readers online. Once attention is captured, the quality of website content turns first impressions into lasting ones.[127]

Electronic Communication

The partners should also establish a system for mass communication. Social media platforms encourage visitors to become followers who then can be contacted as a group. A database can be established from website and social media followers, readers, and individuals from the partners' personal communication files. Mass electronic mailing is appropriate for the announcement of a new product, a book signing, a promotion, highlighting a specific article in a journal, and endeavors whose success is dependent upon the participation of the authors' followers.

Email marketing programs like *MailChimp®* or *Constant Contact®* can deliver a single attractive message to thousands of recipients at the same time. These programs support customized templates that make it easy to craft an email uniquely suited to each campaign. They also allow the organization of the database into meaningful groups so that authors can tailor communication for specific cohorts.

Social Media

In the 21st century, social media has replaced traditional media as the primary influencer of young people.[123] Involvement in *Facebook®, Twitter®, Instagram®, Pinterest®, Tumblr®, SnapChat®*, or similar platforms can facilitate a personal and instant connection with potential readers. A consistent and engaging online presence requires planning, resources, and commitment.

Posts on social media serve to engage readers and establish a following for the products developed by the partnership. Communication on social media platforms is crafted primarily around conversation, including promotions and sales efforts.[128] Images engage readers' attention and can be used effectively both on social media platforms and on the partnership's website. Memes, humorous images, or videos are easy to craft and can make repeated messages appear new and engaging.

Each social media platform has a different communication style, focus, and target audience. *Instagram®* and *Snapchat®* target a younger audience whose communication style is rapid and who are less concerned with the longevity of information. *Twitter®*, with a limit of 280 characters, is a vehicle for posting short messages or announcements in real time. The *LinkedIn®* platform is designed for business and career professionals to network with one another. *Facebook®*, where postings are easily accessible, has a broad audience in terms of age, education, and socioeconomic status. Young adult readers (Millennials), compared to senior adults (Boomers and older), have a less restrictive interpretation of personal boundaries and privacy and share their thoughts and activities more readily on public platforms than their elder colleagues.

Campaigns to increase site exposure often call upon loyal followers to share a message. A posting on the partnership's Facebook page that is shared by followers can reach thousands of individuals in a matter of minutes. *Facebook®* also provides the option of author pages for showcasing and promoting the partners' products.

Nearly all of the social media platforms have incorporated mechanisms to support online purchases, providing authors with a convenient avenue for book or article promotion and sales. Rewarding loyal readers with an incentive such as a discount on purchases or a free download of some kind can promote retention.

Building an online presence is a time-consuming endeavor that requires planning and a budget. The partnership's online marketing plan might begin with building a website and establishing one social media platform at a time, with the goal of developing a following and maximizing its potential before expending resources on additional platforms. The need to connect with the greatest number of readers competes with the need to concentrate on writing. If the partnership has sufficient resources, engaging the assistance of external team members in marketing efforts would increase the amount of time available to write.

Conclusion

Marketing is a broad-based initiative that combines the various components of product, place, promotion, and price in a coordinated effort both to meet the readers' needs and to sell the partnership's product. Authors should address the marketing plan early in the development of a product as it influences the project as well as promotion and sales. Marketing requires a communication platform that allows the partners to promote their product and share information with large numbers of people. The communication platform, at a minimum, should include an author website, a program for email marketing, and a presence on social media.

8

CREATIVITY

Consider Creativity an important factor when evaluating product development and author integrity. For example, are the authors true to themselves; does the writing respect their own moral boundaries; does the content remain consistent with the setting, the characters/participants, and the culture of the work. The fiction author must remain true to the point of view of the character (the character's *voice*), ensuring that what the character says and does is consistent with who and what he or she is. Embrace the diversity of the partnership by encouraging the partners to bounce ideas off one another. By fostering creativity in the development of their products, partners can explore their own artistic talent.

8.1 Writing can be creative and fun. On the scale in Figure 8.1 with Fun (i.e. creative, self-indulgent, novel, expressive) on one end and Work (i.e. business side of writing, dissemination, publish or perish, making money) at the other, place an **X** on the line to represent your current position in your project, then explain your position to your partner. Understanding your partner's interpretation of work adds to your knowledge about one another and strengthens the partnership.

Figure 8.1: Writing Fun - Work Scale© (Baker & Goodman)

Do the partners' *Xs* fall in approximately the same location or are they noticeably distant from one another? Do they interpret work and fun in the same way? It is not unusual for one person to enjoy a task that another finds arduous. Do one or both need to adjust their thinking to promote an environment that supports each partner's independent and collective creativity?[129]

Designing creative, time-limited activities in a low-risk environment will generate a sense of urgency without pressure or stress. For example, a 1-minute writing exercise promotes spontaneity because it does not allow time for pondering details. The exercise can produce imaginative and unanticipated outcomes.

When there is pressure, such as an impending deadline, the environment can become stressful. Stress transitions the environment from low-risk to high-risk, diminishing creativity and producing outcomes that are less valuable. A high-risk environment may cause the partners to settle on an outcome that pleases no one. Avoid undue stress by taking the time to play, have fun, and dream with the writing, which promotes a meaningful and successful outcome. (Figure 8.2).

Figure 8.2: Steps to Success

> **Success**
>
> If you can dream it,
>   you can assess it.
>
> If you can assess it,
>   you can determine the goal.
>
> If you can determine the goal,
>   you can establish an action plan.
>
> If you can establish an action plan,
>   you can implement the plan.
>
> If you can implement the plan,
>   you can evaluate the outcomes.
>
> If you can evaluate the outcomes,
>   you are SUCCESSFUL!

*Permission to use granted
by J.D. Baker, May 27, 2018*

Ethics

While exercising creativity, authors must be true to ethical values. Ethics means *doing the right thing,* yet there can be more than one right way of doing anything. Ethical behavior among the partners is straightforward; but, ethics in writing can be easy to describe, but harder to implement. Greenberg[130] points out that laws governing defamation, libel, harassment, and hate speech demonstrate that words can be hurtful and damaging. Authoring involves responsibility and choice. Authors must establish acceptable limits and weigh the effect of their words on the reader. They must avoid prejudice related to what people *are unable to change* while exploring the reality of individuals and their behavior without prejudice.[130]

The ethical challenge for authors is an "effort to reconcile truth and beauty"[130] or balance the reality of the story with the richness of description. In non-fiction, the authors must remain true to the facts when developing a narrative to convey the logic of a situation. However, authors are afforded *poetic* license, the right to deliver the content in their own words. For example, "a *plausible impossibility* is more pleasing than *what is implausible but possible.*" ... "In both cases, beauty (aesthetics) trumps truth (ethics)."[130] The author finds pleasure in the act of telling a story by creating astonishment for the reader and plausibility for the narrative.[130]

Staying true to the *voice* of each character is integral to storytelling, especially in writing fiction where the author creates the framework in which the story takes place. A story happens when a character does or says something that has consequences.[130] Stories can create astonishment when outcomes are contrary to expectations, or they can cause the reader to ponder the ethics of a situation or the vagaries of nature. Authors strive to *show, not tell* by choosing words that help readers visualize details that are not specified, and imagine what is happening without a great deal of explanation.[130]

In fiction, the narrative must be consistent with the character's personality and role. The ethical challenge for the author is *how* to tell the story. For example, although profanity is generally not appreciated in a narrative, it *may* be consistent with a character's mode of expression and appropriate when the character is speaking. However, the author must consider the target reader and choose the narrative that is both consistent with the character's *voice* and the sensitivities of the reader. Consider how the age of the target audience will inform the author's handling of romance and a sexual encounter, avoiding explicit description for an audience not yet mature enough for that level of detail.

ADDIE Model

The ADDIE model[131,132] (Figure 8.3). (Analysis, Design, Development, Implementation, Evaluation) is a curriculum developmental tool that has merit for exploring creativity within a writing partnership. Partners can use the model as a framework to produce a journal article or a book of fiction or non-fiction.

Figure 8.3: Addie Model[131,132]

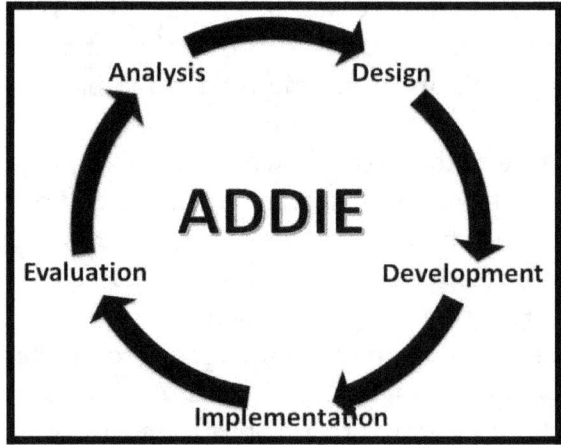

Analysis

During analysis, the authors explore the goal or purpose of their project and create specific objectives for measuring success. They identify the problem; for example, in fiction, they determine the crisis that the main character will face. For a research article, they clarify the purpose of the study and identify the gap in the literature that their study addresses. Then they define the goals and the objectives[131,132] and additional elements to explore in the development of the manuscript. Authors explore journal options for disseminating an article, seek publishing options for a book of fiction or non-fiction, and agree upon project deadlines.

8.2 Consider the following set of sample questions during the analysis phase:

- Who are the target readers? How old are they? What type of work do they do? Are they predominately male or female? What are their interests?
- What is the desired outcome for the reader? For example, for
- fiction: the outcome might be the enjoyment of losing oneself in time, in the story, or the desire to read the upcoming novels in a series.
- non-fiction: the outcome might be to alter practice based on the knowledge gained from the work.
- What constraints exist? (e.g., reading level or language barriers if distributing the work worldwide)
- What are the delivery options? (Print book, electronic book, journal article).
- What deadlines does the partnership face?
- Are there monetary or other penalties or consequences for not meeting the deadline?[132]

Design

Design incorporates the authors' creative content, writing style, and format. For journals, the required format is described in the author guidelines. Deciding early upon the use of first or third person can prevent rework; all authors begin with the same directions. Attention to detail is imperative in the design phase.[131]

Development

The Development phase includes gathering support materials and completing the first draft of the manuscript. For journal articles and books, authors implement a repeating series of *review, edit, review, edit* and solicit external reviewers for the product. The Development phase ends with the completion of the manuscript, including the final edits.[131,132]

Implementation

The implementation phase begins with submitting the manuscript for publication. Journal articles require peer review and editing, a process that is managed by the publisher and repeated until the manuscript is ready for publication. Implementation includes ensuring that any required elements for submission are included: permission to use images or graphics, any releases, signing of the author copyright transfer agreement. The finished book or article is converted into the print or electronic format indicated in the Design phase. All materials (manuscript, graphics, photos, testimonials, etc.) should be gathered into one location for uploading into the publication platform.[131,132] The final step in implementation is the printing of the publication and dissemination of the work.

Evaluation

The Evaluation phase consists of both *formative* and *summative* evaluations. Formative evaluation is designed to review and improve the product during development. Approaches include having the partners read and edit one another's work, then clarify through discussion and negotiation. Beta readers can provide valuable insight from a target reader viewpoint. Formative evaluation can be implemented as frequently as is practical.

Summative evaluation, comprising opportunities for readers to provide feedback and for partners to track exposure and sales, occurs once the product has been published.[131,132] For books, summative evaluation includes the number and quality of reader reviews, comments on social media, sales figures, and recognition or awards. For journal articles, a summative evaluation may be the number of times other authors cite the work in their publications.

Time Allocation

Allocating time to each ADDIE element keeps the project on track.[133] Table 8.4 provides a suggestion for allocating a percentage of time for each phase of the ADDIE process.

Table 8.4: Partner Writing Project (% of Time)

Partner Writing Project (% of Time)
Analyze (10%) • Develop target reader profile • Select a journal if the product is an article. • Determine project format (print &/or electronic) • Identify the goal of the project and incremental objectives for determining success • Create an outline, proposal, scene list, initial literature search, etc. • Determine delivery & assessment strategies • Seek formative feedback from your partner &/or obtain sign-off
Design (35%) • Determine key components of evaluation or metrics • Select a shared/networking platform such as *DropBox®* or *Google® Docs*. • Make writing assignments for each partner. • Determine frequency and location for backing up the partner's work and decide who will be responsible for that task. • Seek formative feedback and/or agreement from your partner.

Develop (40%)
- Write, write, write.
- Review with your partner.
- Edit, edit, edit. (write/review/edit is a repeating process for as long as needed).
- Develop a formative feedback form for beta readers or external reviewers.
- Edit work based on the feedback.
- Seek formative feedback and/or agreement from your partner of a larger project team.
- Attend to any revision requests made by peer reviewers/editor.

Implement (5%)
- Create a cover design if a book.
- Submit for publication or prepare for self-publishing or seek an agent if pursuing traditional publishing.
- Implement promotional strategies (book).

Evaluate (10%)
- Consider all metrics identified in the Design phase (e.g., number of citations in selected which journals or number of books sold).
- Gather summative feedback from readers, partner, project team, employer.
- Interpret evaluation data for improvement opportunities.

Become a *Creative Giant*, who is naturally compassionate and creative and has "the vision to see how the world might be, the courage to take action, and the capability to actually change the world."[134] Plan well and use available time wisely.

Practice Writing as an Artist

A partnership writing project is an *enhanced scaffolding*[135] process in which the partners begin with an idea, develop characters, explore options for plot development, and determine how it all comes together. Journal guidelines detail the scaffolding for articles. Journal editors and publishers provide a style guide detailing elements such as margin width, font size, the frequency of formative review and critique among partners that help to ensure a robust manuscript. Kim[135] found students who received enhanced scaffolding instructions displayed higher critical thinking levels as authors and peer editors. Scaffolding also helps with consistency of format while partners work both independently and collaboratively on platforms such as *DropBox®* or *Google Docs®*.

Pictographic Illustrations

Scott[136] recommended using *pictographic illustrations* like street signs as imaginative prompts to aid in generating ideas. Creative exercises can also be valuable for partners as they craft their manuscript. (Figure 8.5). For works of fiction, reorganizing the illustrations may generate new ideas for theme and plot development.[137] For non-fiction, illustrations clarify and augment the content with visual representation.

8.3 Copy a set of images like those below for each partner. Cut them apart and reorder them to create a story.

A, B, & Cs of Author Partnering

Figure 8.5: Street Sign Image Examples

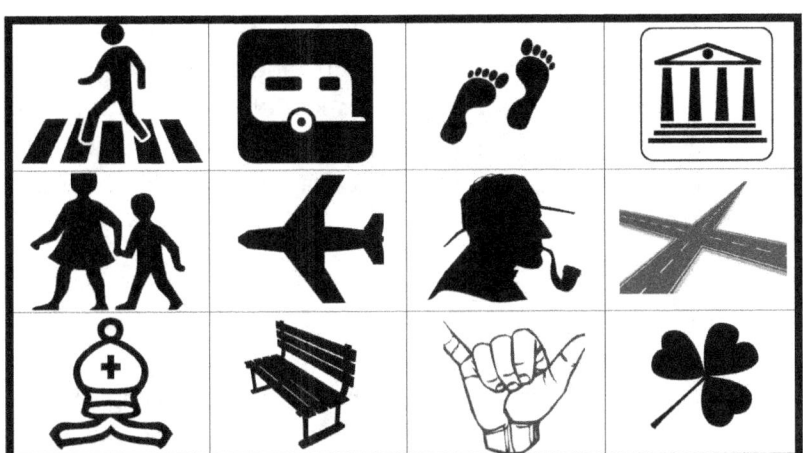

Created by Baker & Goodman with individual images from *Creative Commons for commercial use and editable.*

One way for partners to develop a storyline is to take the same set of images, organize them independently, then share their creations with one another. This exercise can transition into a storyboard with a column of images with corresponding text. Comparing and sharing their individual narratives can stimulate a variety of ideas from which a story outline can emerge.

8.4 Another approach is for each partner to create images (stick figures are fine) on 3x3 inch sticky notes. Each partner generates 10-30 graphics that represent the work the partners are developing. First, independently, and then collaboratively they organize the sticky notes into storylines, creating a mind-map or outline for the story, and leading the storyline that best represents their goal.

Lifeline

The partners can use a pictorial lifeline, either about themselves or about their story to share ideas with one another. The lifeline depicts highs and lows and spotlights key elements in the narrative. Lifelines do not have to be drawn in a linear fashion; they can be circles, arcs, spirals, etc. Encourage one another other to think outside the proverbial box.

8.5.1 Create your personal lifeline using graphics to represent significant milestones. Lifelines can be developed any way you choose, linear, circular, spiral, arc, squiggly line, etc. Think outside the colloquial box. Then, write a 500-word narrative (approximately two pages) that tells your story. Read one another's stories. Discuss what you have learned about each another and about the creative process.

8.5.2 Study the lifeline in Figure 8.6, then independently write 500 words narrating this person's story. Exchange stories with your partner, discussing the similarities and differences in your writing styles and other characteristics of the stories you created.

Figure 8.6: Story Lifeline

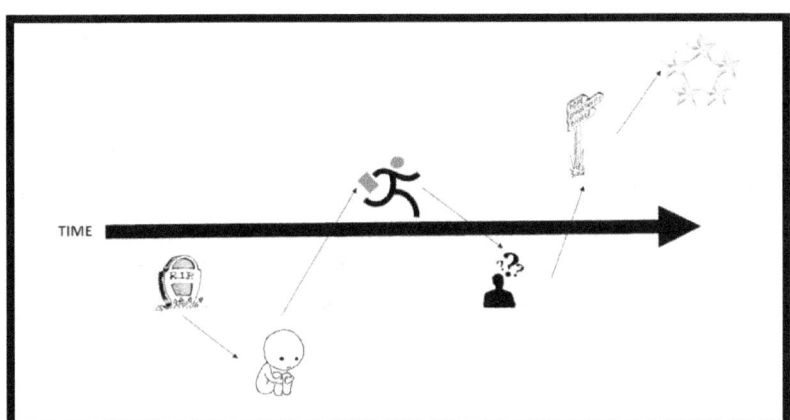

Created by Baker & Goodman with individual images from
Creative Commons for commercial use and editable.

Creating art, including writing, combines genius and the ability to learn.[137] Developing a creative identity involves three elements: (a) immersing oneself without fear of judgment; (b) being willing to take risks; and (c) incorporating self-reflection and creative problem-solving. The third step requires a willingness to critique one's own work and to seek feedback from external reviewers. Formal and technical elements of writing can be learned, but technique must be augmented with vision and creativity to produce a work that is original and creative.[137]

Creativity is the muse that elevates a work to dimensions beyond flat and restrictive. The spirit of creativity spurs a chain reaction that *enlivens and quickens* the imagination yielding *purposive momentum*.[137] Creativity requires persistence and a willingness to view the work with a critical eye while allowing playful imagination to soar. The process of creating can be hard work and messy, but at the same time, fun! Finding enjoyment in writing can spur the team to achieve outcomes that exceed expectations. Making time for play and fun, particularly in the early phases of writing, can contribute to the social and cultural world the authors are creating for themselves and their characters and readers.[138]

Critique should not occur until the creation is complete. Authors should distance themselves from the completed manuscript in order to review it objectively. Rereading it after time has elapsed allows them to reflect and revise. Writers benefit from feedback when potential readers review the narrative. For fiction, that process may involve a group of beta readers; for scholarly works, reviewers may include other members of the research team, the journal's peer reviewers, and editors.

Conclusion

Co-creating can be fun, exciting, and can lead to a successful book or article. As part of working together, writing partners develop an ethical understanding of themselves and their work. The ADDIE model can be used for developing and organizing a writing plan, creating the manuscript, keeping the project on track, and facilitating a stellar outcome. If partners need a boost to free their creativity, they can draw pictures, use mind-maps, and brainstorm with one another to stimulate the free flow of thoughts and ideas. Most of all, have fun with writing.

9

CALL TO ACTION

Throughout this book, we have proposed strategies for developing an effective foundation for writing as partners. Now it is time to begin the journey that will lead to a published work. Consider the components of author partnering explored throughout this book. Choose your partner(s) wisely; ensure that your partnership has the skill mix required to take the project from concept to publication. Use the *A, B, & Cs of Author Partnering* as a blueprint to develop the infrastructure that facilitates your success.

9.1 Record your responses to each element below to establish a realistic plan for meeting the writing obligations you and your partner establish.

- Choose the date on which you will begin writing.

- Commit to a deadline to complete the manuscript.
- Determine the number of words to write each day.
- Decide the number of days per week you will write.

Share the personal commitments you made to the partnership with a confidant. This may be a close friend or spouse who will motivate, mentor, and support you throughout the process and help to keep you on track. Establish a check-in or reporting routine so your confidant can remind you if there is something you have missed. Having a support system (cheerleader, advisor, or sounding board) in place fosters forward momentum.

Develop a healthy respect for structure, timeframes, and process. Create a realistic timeline that accounts for all the activities and milestones required to achieve the goal. Consider work-life balance and identify personal conflicting obligations and expectations that may influence the time available for the writing project. Create a contract that documents expectations and commitments. Develop a realistic writing schedule and stick to it, reviewing and editing until the manuscript is complete. Build the external team of experts needed to complete the writing project.

9.2 Use this checklist in the workbook to review the essential elements of each chapter in the *A, B, & Cs of Author Partnering*.

Do not permit timidity or inertia to stand in the way of your success.

Be sure to include opportunities for celebration!

WORKBOOK

Alignment

Name: _____   Date: _____

Exercise 1.1

Answer the following questions individually and then collectively discuss responses.

1. **What do I personally want to get out of this project?**
2. **Why am I here?**
3. **What will the project do for me personally/ professionally?**
4. **How will this project change my**   a. **life?**   b. **work?**   c. **family?**
5. **What will I commit to the project?**
6. **What am I willing to sacrifice for the project?**
7. **What do I want to walk away with if we dissolve our partnership?**

Exercise 1.2

Answer the following questions individually and then collectively discuss responses.

1. **Why do I want to work with this partner?**
2. **What does this partner bring to the table?** *(perhaps that I don't, won't, or can't)*
3. **What do I value most in my partner?**
4. **How do I support my partner when we face challenges (i.e. slow progress, slumps, writer's block, or external pressures)?**
5. **How can my partner support me when we face similar challenges?**

Exercise 1.3

Partners should agree to listen first and explore all aspects of an issue before making a final decision. They should set a standard early in the partnership that ensures the partners seek the best means to remain aligned by leaving no conflict unresolved.

Answer the following questions individually and then collectively discuss responses.

1. To whom are we committed?

2. What role does transparency play in our partnership?

3. What steps will we take to ensure transparency?

4. How will we
• demonstrate diversity? • demonstrate our commitment to ensuring that no conflict remains unresolved? • manage conflicting priorities?

Exercise 1.4

Complete the form individually then share your answers with your partner to explore disparities and create new ideas.

1. **What is the purpose or primary goal of the project?**

2. **What specific contributions do I bring to the project?**
• Knowledge   • Skill   • Experience

3. **Whom will this project serve?**

4. **How will the target audience benefit?**

5. **What is the best format to meet the target readers' needs?**
☐ **Journal article:** New practice? Solution to a problem? Fill a gap in the literature?   ☐ **Book:** Fiction or non-fiction?

6. **How long should this project take?**

7. **Why am I willing to invest time and effort?**

S.M.A.R.T. Exercise 1.5

Using the S.M.A.R.T. framework[1] below seek consensus by responding individually to the questions, then share and discuss the responses to develop an agreed-upon overarching goal statement for the project. The tool may also be used for intermediate goals as the writing progresses.

Initial Goal: Record the primary goal identified in Exercise 1.4.

1. **S**pecific:

    a. What is/are the specific goal(s) targeted for accomplishment?

    b. Why is the goal personally important? Be specific about what achieving the goal means both to individual and to the partnership.

    c. Use the answers to who, what, when, where, why, and how, to develop the overarching project goal.

2. **M**easurable:

    a. Record specifically what the outcome will look like when completed.

    b. How will goal progress be evaluated?

3. **A**chievable:

    a. What is the partner's shared motivation to accomplish the goal?

    b. Are the skills needed available within the partnership? If not, will the partners develop the skills or solicit them from external team members?

c. Are the partner's assignments balanced fairly and appropriately assigned based on skills needed to achieve the goal?

4. **R**elevant: *Determine whether each objective is aligned with the project goal. If not, what will it take to adjust them?*

5. **T**ime-bound: *Establish realistic deadlines.*

Edit the Goal: *Does the goal need editing based on the responses to this exercise?*

Balance

Exercise 2.1

Work-life balance is unique to each person. *What is most important to you regarding work-life balance? Respond to the following questions and complete the worksheet on the next page. Consider sharing the results with your partner.*

- If I were to die today, what would I say were the top three **accomplishments** or outcomes in my life? The list created addresses your personal values.

- From the six **core values:** (a) Sense of Self, (b) Achievement, (c) Intimacy, (d) Creativity & Play, (e) Search for Meaning, and (f) Compassion and Contribution, determine the one best associated with each accomplishment. If more than one core value fits an accomplishment, select the one that represents the *best* fit.

- Record the **functional area:** (a) Work, (b) Professional: Career Development or Service, (c) Interpersonal Relationships: Couples, Families, Friends (d) Personal: Self-care, health & nutrition, spiritual, where each of the accomplishments listed took place.

- Using the three, **dimension level** scales: (a) Time, (b) Satisfaction, and (c) Involvement, place an X to indicate whether you spent more or less time on each accomplishment related to all work-life activities you were engaged at the time.

Now that you have completed this with what you have already accomplished in your life, repeat the process with **what you will accomplish** in the next year, 5-years, and 10-years. Thinking forward based on what you have learned about your values, function areas, and dimension levels.

A, B, & Cs of Author Partnering

Accomplishments, Core Values, and Dimension Levels

Past Accomplishment

#	1. Record top 3-Accomplishments Accomplishment	#	2. Record Core Value Core Value	#	3. Record Functional Functional Area	Dimension Level	4. Mark an X on the scale Less　　　　　More
1		1.1		1.2		Time Satisfaction Involvement	|---------|---------| |---------|---------| |---------|---------|
2		2.1		2.2		Time Satisfaction Involvement	|---------|---------| |---------|---------| |---------|---------|
3		3.1		3.2		Time Satisfaction Involvement	|---------|---------| |---------|---------| |---------|---------|

Planned Accomplishments Next Year

#	1. Record top 3-Accomplishments Accomplishment	#	2. Record Core Value Core Value	#	3. Record Functional Functional Area	Dimension Level	4. Mark an X on the scale Less　　　　　More
1		1.1		1.2		Time Satisfaction Involvement	|---------|---------| |---------|---------| |---------|---------|
2		2.1		2.2		Time Satisfaction Involvement	|---------|---------| |---------|---------| |---------|---------|
3		3.1		3.2		Time Satisfaction Involvement	|---------|---------| |---------|---------| |---------|---------|

Planned Accomplishments (bucket list) 5-years

#	1. Record top 3-Accomplishments Accomplishment	#	2. Record Core Value Core Value	#	3. Record Functional Functional Area	Dimension Level	4. Mark an X on the scale Less　　　　　More
1		1.1		1.2		Time Satisfaction Involvement	|---------|---------| |---------|---------| |---------|---------|
2		2.1		2.2		Time Satisfaction Involvement	|---------|---------| |---------|---------| |---------|---------|
3		3.1		3.2		Time Satisfaction Involvement	|---------|---------| |---------|---------| |---------|---------|

Planned Accomplishments (bucket list) 10-years

#	1. Record top 3-Accomplishments Accomplishment	#	2. Record Core Value Core Value	#	3. Record Functional Area Functional Area	Dimension Level	4. Mark an X on the scale Less　　　　　More
1		1.1		1.2		Time Satisfaction Involvement	|---------|---------| |---------|---------| |---------|---------|
2		2.1		2.2		Time Satisfaction Involvement	|---------|---------| |---------|---------| |---------|---------|
3		3.1		3.2		Time Satisfaction Involvement	|---------|---------| |---------|---------| |---------|---------|

Exercise 2.2

Think about your involvement in the writing partnership and record your answers.

1.	How willing are you to commit the **time** required to achieve the goal? Expand on the response.
2.	Will the work provide a level of **satisfaction** that allows you to make the goal of the partnership a priority? Expand on the response.
3.	What level of **involvement** in decision-making related to the partnership activities do you want? Expand on the response.
4.	Are you willing to adjust the **time** that you are involved in other activities that may be preventing you from accomplishing your desired level of **satisfaction** and **involvement** in the partnership? Expand on the response.
5.	What can you give up that will represent little or no sacrifice, to free up **time** for the work of the partnership?

Exercise 2.3

From this list of motivational factors, rank your top three?

Hygiene Factors:	Satisfiers:
• Working conditions • Policies and administration practices • Compensation • Relationship among partners • Job security • Personal life	• Recognition • Achievement • Advancement • Growth • Responsibility • Job challenge

Record the answers to the following questions to identify and clarify partners' motivational level.[16]

1. **What is going well?**

2. **What values in life are important to you?**

3. **What aspects of the partnership are important to you?**

4. **What gives you the most enjoyment?**

5. **What are the barriers you perceive to a more satisfying partnership?**

6. **Is there someone or something in your life that is stopping you from achieving your highest level of satisfaction?**

7. **How can you covert these barriers to opportunities?**

8. **Who is your writing ally? Who helps keep you on schedule?**

9. **Whom do you need to meet or connect to further your ideas?**

Exercise 2.4

Test offline skill development for one week. Place your phone on airplane mode, do not open email, nor access social media, for at least one hour a day and prohibit phone use during meals.

- **Record what you have accomplished related to managing work priorities by using this technique.**

- **Review the week to see how effective your work-life balance activities have progressed, for example, test the "no phone use during meals." Is there a sense of increased control by using this technique?**

- **Reflect on the increased control compared to succumbing to immediately responding to interruptions that previously disrupted workflow. Assess the difference in the quality of family interaction and note reduction in disruptions.**

Commitment

Exercise 3.1

On the scale below mark with an X your level of commitment to the partnership then record your rationale for the placement for each scale.

Personal: Where does your willingness to commit to the partnership fall on the scale?

Continuance: Where does your appreciation for the benefits you gain from the partnership fall on the scale?

Normative: Where does your feeling of obligation to the partnership fall on the scale?

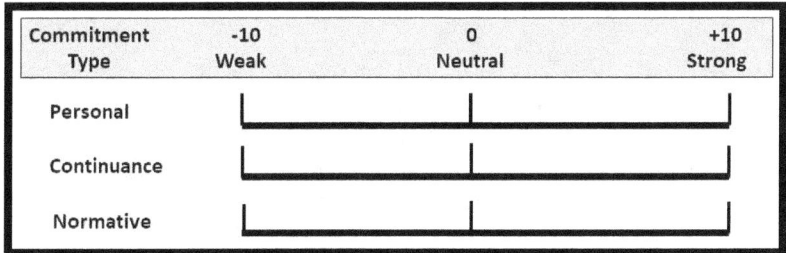

RATIONALE for each score:

- **Personal**

- **Continuance**

- **Normative**

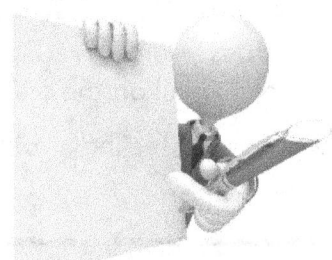

Contract

Contract Resources

Go to these sites to find sample contracts and additional resources.

Sample Contracts:
- http://jamesaconrad.com/writing/author-collaboration.html[50]
- https://selfpubauthors.wordpress.com/2011/12/20/a-sample-co-author-contact/[51]

Additional Resources
- Recommendations related to forming a partnership[52] http://www.dmlp.org/legal-guide/forming-partnership
- 50-State Guide to Forming a Partnership[53] https://www.nolo.com/legal-encyclopedia/50-state-guide-establishing-general-partnership.html
- How to Make a Business a Partnership when a Partner Lives in Another State[54] https://info.legalzoom.com/make-business-partnership-partner-lives-another-state-22480.html
- Learn about the Specifics of a Partnership[55] https://www.thebalancesmb.com/what-should-be-included-in-a-partnership-agreement-398879

Exercise 4.1

Answer the following questions to determine elements for inclusion in your contract.[44]

1. **What is the purpose/goal of the partnership?**
2. **How will each partner contribute to the goal?**
3. **When will the work be completed?**
4. **How will the product(s) be evaluated?**
5. **How will a tie be broken?**
6. **How will author order be established?**

7. **Who will be the corresponding partner** *(communicate and negotiate with external team members)*?
8. **What expenses will the partnership cover?**
9. **Who will manage the partnership finances?**
10. **How will proceeds be shared?**
11. **What is the dissolution strategy**?

Communication

Exercise 5.1.a

Focus on different aspects of the partnership that are dependent on different styles of effective communication.

1. **List various aspects of partnering such as editing, planning a meeting, communicating with external team members, etc. and discuss the communication styles most appropriate for each.**

2. **What communication style(s) should your partner have to complement yours?**

Exercise 5.1.b

Communicating with your partner, a journal editor, external team members, and your readers requires effective communication. Craft communication for each of the following circumstances. Remember to be clear, concise, truthful to build credibility, include appropriate facts, examples or stories for clarification.

1. **Create a query letter to a journal editor**
2. **Solicit a graphic artist for cover design.**
3. **Negotiate price-point of your novel with your partner. Determine what information they need.**
4. **Create examples specific to your own partnership and product.**

Conflict Resolution

Exercise 6.1

Record your **P**referred and **S**econdary styles on the Figure below, then discuss with your partner.

Figure 2 Developed from Blake and Mouton's content.[95]

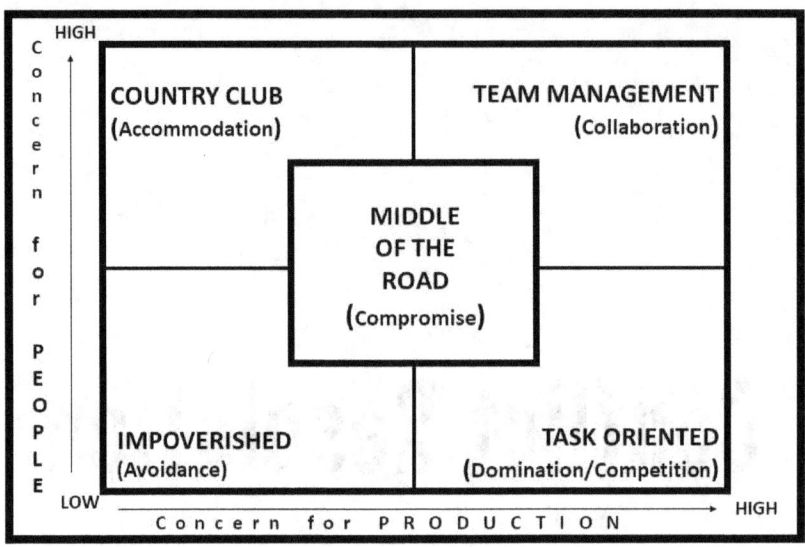

Commerce

Exercise 7.1

Record your strategies surrounding the 4Ps of Marketing.

PRODUCT	PLACE

PROMOTION	PRICE

Creativity

Exercise 8.1

Mark an **X** *on the creativity scale below to indicate your position in your current project.*

Share your interpretation of your position with your partner.

Figure 3: Writing Fun - Work Scale© (Baker & Goodman)

Do the partners' **X**s fall in approximately the same location or are they noticeably distant from one another?

Do they interpret work and fun in the same way?

It is not unusual for one person to enjoy a task that another finds arduous. Do one or both need to adjust their thinking to promote an environment that supports each partner's independent and collective creativity?[129]

Exercise 8.2

Using the ADDIE Model record your responses below relative to the Analysis phase.

Figure 8.3: Addie Model[131,132]

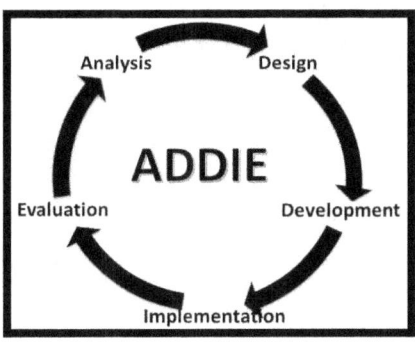

ANALYSIS[132]
1. **Who is the target reader, profession, etc.? How old are they? What type of work do they do? Are they predominately male or female? What are their interests?**
2. **What is the desired outcome for the reader? For example, for**
o fiction, the outcome might be the enjoyment of losing oneself in time, in the story, or the desire to read the upcoming novels in a series.   o non-fiction, it might be to alter practice based on the knowledge gained from the work.

3.	**What constraints exist (e.g., reading level or language barriers if distributing the work worldwide)?**
4.	**What are the delivery options? (Print book, electronic book, journal article)**
5.	**What deadlines does the partnership face?**
6.	**Are there monetary or other penalties or consequences of not meeting the deadline?**

Exercise 8.3

Create a story with the images below. Copy a set for each partner, cut the images apart, and reorder the images to tell the story.

Figure 8.5: Street Sign Image Examples (Created by Baker & Goodman with individual images from *Creative Commons for commercial use and editable*).

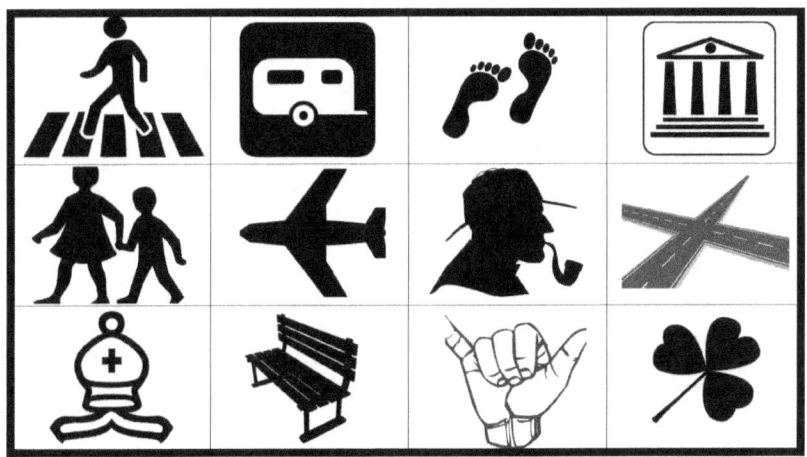

Exercise 8.4

Each partner creates 10-30 images or graphics (stick figures are fine) on 3x3 inch sticky notes that support the project ideas. Share the created images, then both independently and collaboratively organize them into a single storyline.

The resulting graphics become a mind-map or outline for the project.

Exercise 8.5.1

Create your personal lifeline on this page. Be as creative as possible. Lifelines can be developed any way you choose, linear, circular, spiral, arc, squiggly line, etc. Think outside the colloquial box. Then write 500 words that tell your story and share with your partner. Discuss what each of you learned about allowing yourself to be creative.

Exercise 8.5.2

Write 500 words to tell a story based on this person's lifeline.

Figure 8.6: Story Lifeline (Created by Baker & Goodman with individual images from *Creative Commons for commercial use and editable.*

Call to Action

Exercise 9.1

Complete the following pledge.

I will begin writing by _____ (date).

I will write _____ words each day for _____ days a week until my part is completed on time by_____.

Exercise 9.2

*Place an **X** in the box next to each item as you and your partner complete each task.*

Table 9.1 Partner Checklist

X	TASK
ALIGNMENT	
	Identify the purpose or primary goal of the project.
	Make a purposeful selection of Partner(s) based on knowledge and skills (contribution to partnership).
	Establish goals and objectives.
	Determine the author order.
	Identify the division of labor among partners: financial management, the corresponding representative with external partners; manuscript editing; website development; blog development; social media management, etc.
	Establish conflict management strategies.
BALANCE	
	Determine both partnership and individual partners' values.
	Define motivational requirements.
	Explore work-life balance.
	Negotiate conflicting personal obligations (both within and external to the partnership).
	Establish schedules, timeframes, and deadlines.
	Define critical project elements.
COMMITMENT	
	Define commitment to the project.
	Define commitment to partner(s).
	Negotiate variances in partners' perceptions and recommendations.

	Locate/hire the external partners required to complete the project.
CONTRACT	
	Negotiate the terms of the partnership contract.
	Sign the agreement.
COMMERCE: THE ART OF MARKETING	
	Become part of the writing community; join writers' organizations; participate in events; make a name for yourself.
	Create and manage a marketing plan that addresses: • Product • Place • Promotion • Price
	Create and manage a website.
	Write and publish a blog.
	Create and manage a social media platform.
	Establish a communication database.
CONFLICT RESOLUTION	
	Implement pre-established strategies to address conflict.
	Welcome diversity.
CREATIVITY	
	Work through the ADDIE Model with the project
CALL TO ACTION	
WRITE, WRITE, & WRITE	
	Complete your manuscript.
	Submit for Publication.
	Do not permit timidity or inertia to stand in the way of your success.
!!!!CELEBRATE!!!!	

REFERENCES

1. J. Bowman, L. Morgensen, E. Marsland and N. Lannin, "The development, content validity and inter-rater reliability of the SMART-Goal Evaluation Method: A standardised method for evaluating clinical goals," *Australian Occupational Therapy Journal,* vol. 62, pp. 420-427, 2015.
2. A. Dance, "Who's on first?," *Nature,* vol. 489, pp. 591-593, 2012.
3. Marušić-etal., "Five-step authorship framework to improve transparency in disclosing contributor to industry-sponsored clinical trial publications," *BMC Medicine,* vol. 12, p. 197, 2014.
4. K. Rose and J. Anderson, "Top 10 list for building team science," *Research in Gerontological Nursing,* vol. 9, no. 6, pp. 254-255, 2016.
5. ICMJE, "Recommendations for the conduct, reporting, editing, and publication of scholarly works in medical journals.," 2017. [Online]. Available: http://www.icmje.org/recommendations/. [Accessed 6 June 2018].
6. J. D. Baker, "Walking the copyright tightrope," *AORN Journal,* vol. 97, no. 2, pp. 167-171, February 2013.

7. D. Moher, "Along with the privilege of authorship come important responsibilities," *BMC Medicine,* vol. 12, p. 214, 2014.
8. J. Phillippi, F. Likis and E. Tilden, "Authorship grids: Practical tools to facilitate collaboration and ethical publication," *Research in Nursing and Health,* vol. 41, pp. 195-208, 2018.
9. K. B. Gaberson, "Co-author or teacher?," *AORN Journal,* vol. 90, no. 1, pp. 19-22, 2009.
10. N. Chorn, "The alignment theory: Creating strategic fit," *Management Decision,* vol. 29, no. 1, pp. 20-24, 1991.
11. C. Griffin, "Enhancing business partner alignment.," 2010. [Online]. Available: https://www.slideshare.net/guest77aeed/business-partners-alignment. [Accessed 6 June 2018].
12. X. Tian and B. Martin, "Impacting forces on eBook business models development," *Publication Research Quarterly,* vol. 27, pp. 230-246, 2011.
13. B. Sargent, "Surprising self-publishing statistics," 28 July 2014.
14. B. Barblan and A. Bowker, "Growth and maturity in the self-publishing industry," 5 January 2018.
15. J. Smith, "8 ways to achieve better work-life balance," 18 April 2013. [Online]. Available: Https://www.forbes.com/sites/jacquelynsmith/2013/04/18/8-ways-to-achieve-better-work-life-balance/#4b466c76aba4. [Accessed 6 June 2018].
16. U. Byrne, "Work-life balance: Why are we talking about it at all?," *Business Information Review,* vol. 22, no. 1, pp. 53-59, 2005.
17. S. Phipps and L. Prieto, "A discovery of early labor organizations and the women who advocated work-life balance: An ethical perspective," *Journal Business Ethics,* no. 134, pp. 249-261, 2016.
18. E. Stavrou and C. Lerodiakonou, "Entitlement to work-life balance support: Employee/Manager perceptual discrepancies and their effect on outcomes," *Human Resource Management,* vol. 55, no. 5, pp. 845-869, 2016.

[19] F. Hudson, The adult years: Mastering the art of self-renewal, San Francisco, CA: Jossey-Bass, A Wiley Company, 1999.

[20] S. Stovall and J. D. Baker, "A concept analysis of connections relative to the aging adults," *The Journal of Theory Construction & Testing,* vol. 14, no. 2, pp. 54-58, 2010.

[21] J. D. Baker, Meaning-Making: The stories people tell about their decision to relocate late-in-life, Santa Barbara, CA: The Fielding Institute: Dissertation Abstracts International, 61, (01), 560. (UMI No. AAT 9959039), 2000.

[22] L. Bradley, C. Bailey, H. Lingard and K. Brown, "Managing employees' work-life balance: The impact of management on individual well being and productivity," *Clients driving construction innovation: Moving ideas into practice,* pp. 220-224, 2006.

[23] J. Basar and N. Basim, "A cross-sectional survey on consequences of nurses' burnout: Moderating role of oranizational politics," *Journal of Advanced Nursing,* vol. 72, no. 8, pp. 1838-1850, 2016.

[24] Mental Health America, "Work Life Balance," Mental Health America, 2018. [Online]. Available: http://www.mentalhealthamerica.net/work-life-balance. [Accessed 4 June 2018].

[25] A. Kuijk, "Two Factor Theory by Frederick Herzberg," ToolsHero, 2018. [Online]. Available: https://www.toolshero.com/management/two-factor-theory-herzberg. [Accessed 4 June 2018].

[26] A. Zeeman, "Frederick Herzberg," ToolsHero, 2017. [Online]. Available: https://www.tooshero.com/toolsheroes/frederick-herzberg/. [Accessed 4 June 2018].

[27] R. Cacioppe, "Using team - individual reward and recognition strategies to drive organizational success," *Leadership & Organizational Development Journal,* vol. 20, no. 6, pp. 322-331, 1999.

[28] J. Hale, "6 Reasons Why You Should Celebrate Success More With Your Team," 6 September 2016. [Online].

29. H. Deutschendorf, "7 Habits of people who have achieved work-life balance," Fast Company, 2018. [Online]. Available: https://www.fastcompany.com/3047825/7-habits-of-people-who-have-achieved-work-life-balance. [Accessed 4 June 2018].

Available: https://www.linkedin.com/pulse/6-reasons-why-you-should-celebrate-success-more-your-team-jo-hale/. [Accessed 17 August 2018].

30. C. Gilkey, "Email triage: Calm email stress and overwhelm in 30 minutes (or less)," Productive Flourishing, 2009. [Online]. Available: http://www.productiveflouriishing.com/email-triage. [Accessed 15 May 2018].

31. S. J. Adams, "Inequity in social exchange," *Advances in Experimental Social Psychology*, vol. 2, pp. 267-269, 1965.

32. M. Hutchinson and D. Jackson, "The construction and legitimation of workplace bullying in the public sector: Insight into power dynamics and organizational failures in health and social care," *Nursing Inquiry*, no. 1, pp. 13-26, 2015.

33. J. P. Meyer and L. Herscovitch, "Commitment in the workplace: Toward a general model," *Human Resource Management Review*, vol. 11, pp. 299-326, 2001.

34. R. T. Mowday, L. W. Porter and R. M. Steers, "The measurement of organizational commitment," *Journal of Vocational Behavior*, vol. 14, no. 2, pp. 224-247, April 1979.

35. H. L. Angle and J. L. Perry, "An empirical assessment of organizational commitment and organizational effectiveness," *Administrative Science Quarterly*, vol. 26, no. 1, pp. 1-14, Mar 1981.

36. J. P. Meyer and N. J. Allen, "A three-component conceptualization of organizational commitment," *Human Resource Management Review*, vol. 1, no. 1, pp. 61-89, 1991.

37. Meriam Webster, "Meriam Webster online dictionary," June 2018. [Online]. Available: https://www.merriam-webster.com/dictionary/partnership. [Accessed June 2018].

38. H. Reeder, Commit to win, Garden City, New York: Avery, 2014.

39 Global Humanitarian Platform, "Principles of partnership (PoP) - A statement of commitment," International Council of Voluntary Agencies, 2007. [Online]. Available: https://www.icvanetwork.org/principles-partnership-statement-commitment. [Accessed June 2018].

40 B. Sănduleasa and A. Matei, "Gender equality on labor market and work-life balance policies. A sociological approach," *Journal of Research in Gender Studies,* vol. 4, no. 1, pp. 1199-1216, 2014.

41 R. Crompton and C. Lyonette, "Work-life balance in Europe," *Acta Sociologica,* vol. 49, no. 4, pp. 379-393, 2006.

42 F. Hoque and D. Baer, Everything connects: How to transform and lead in the age of creativity, innovation, and sustainability, New York: McGraw Hill, 2014.

43 L. J. Jassin, "CopyLaw.com," The Law Offices of Lloyd J. Jassin, 2010. [Online]. Available: http://www.copylaw.com/new_articles/collab.html. [Accessed 4 July 2018].

44 K. Pawlak, "Before entering a co-authoring relationship, sign a collaboration agreement," Textbook and Academic Authors Association, 11 September 2011. [Online]. Available: https://blog.taaonline.net/2011/09/before-entering-a-co-authoring-relationship-sign-a-collaboration-agreement/. [Accessed 4 July 2018].

45 S. Lifshitz and E. Finkelstein, "A hermeneutic perspective on the interpretation of contracts," *American Business Law Journal,* vol. 54, no. 3, pp. 519-579, Fall 2017.

46 D. Harmon, P. Kim and K. Mayer, "Breaking the letter vs. spirit of the law: How the interpretation of contract violations affects trust and the management of relationships," *Strategic Management Journal,* vol. 36, pp. 497-517, 2015.

47 US Government, "Copyright law of the United States," US Government, 30 June 2016. [Online]. Available: https://www.copyright.gov/title17/92chap1.html. [Accessed 28 November 2018].

48. US Copyright Office, "Copyright law of the United States and related laws contained in Title 17 of the United States Code," in *Circular 92*, US Copyright Office, 2016, pp. 1-370.
49. M. M. Möhring and J. Finch, "Contracts, relationships and innovation in business-to-business exchanges," *Journal of Business & Industrial Marketing*, vol. 30, no. 3/4, pp. 405-413, 2015.
50. J. A. Conrad, "Writers/book authors – Free fill-in-the-blank collaboration contract forms," n.d. [Online]. Available: http://jamesaconrad.com/writing/author-collaboration.html. [Accessed 4 July 2018].
51. S. Beman, "Self-Published authors helping other authors: Advice on wirting, publishing, and book promotion," 20 December 2011. [Online]. Available: https://selfpubauthors.wordpress.com/2011/12/20/a-sample-co-author-contact/. [Accessed 4 July 2018].
52. J. Murray, "Learn about the specifics of a partnership agreement," [Online]. Available: https://www.thebalancesmb.com/what-should-be-included-in-a-partnership-agreement-398879. [Accessed 20 October 2018].
53. D. Fitzpatrick, "50-state guide for forming a partnership," NOLO, [Online]. Available: https://www.nolo.com/legal-encyclopedia/50-state-guide-establishing-general-partnership.html. [Accessed 20 October 2018].
54. L. Roberts, "How to make a business a partnership when a partner lives in another state," legalzoom, [Online]. Available: https://info.legalzoom.com/make-business-partnership-partner-lives-another-state-22480.html. [Accessed 20 October 2018].
55. J. Murray, "Learn about the specifics of a partnership," The Balance Small Business, [Online]. Available: https://www.thebalancesmb.com/what-should-be-included-in-a-partnership-agreement-398879. [Accessed 20 October 2018].

56 L. J. Jassin and S. C. Schecter, The copyright permission and libel handbook., New York: Wiley, 1998.

57 H. Sedwick, Self-publisher's legal handbook: The step-by-step guide to the legal issues of self-publishing, Santa Rosa, CA: Ten Gallon Press, 2014.

58 A. E. Quinn, "Effective communication in a time of connectivity: An interview with Dr. Beverly Helms," pp. 6-10, Spring 2014.

59 K. Cooper-Duffy and K. Eaker, "Effective team practices: Interprofessional contributions to communication issues with a parent's perspective," *American Journal of Speech-Language Pathology,* vol. 26, pp. 181-192, 2017.

60 Careers Group, "Career consultant coach, The careers group, Royal Holloway University of London," 21 March 2015. [Online]. Available: https://www.thefreelibrary.com/Mastering+workplace+communication%3A+OT+speaks+to+careers+consultant+at...-a0407109960.

61 A. Blanche, "Atlassian blog," 31 May 2017. [Online]. Available: https://www.atlassian.com/blog/inside-atlassian/how-to-navigate-diverse-communication-styles-at-work.

62 W. M. Marston, Emotions of normal people, London: Kegan Paul, Trench, Trubner & Co, Ltd | New York: Harcourt, Brace and Company, 1928.

63 Business Productivity, "Communicate effectively leveraging DISC profiles," 16 September 2013. [Online]. Available: https://www.businessproductivity.com/communicate-effectively-leveraging-disc-profiles/. [Accessed 4 September 2018].

64 A. Cox, "Increasing purposeful communication in the workplace: Two school-district models," *Delta Kappa Gamma Bulletin,* no. Spring, pp. 34-38, 2014.

65 J. Whitlock and M. Purington, "Positive communication strategies. The practical matters series," 2013. [Online]. Available: http://www.selfinjury.bctr.cornell.edu/documents/pm_positive_comm.pdf.

66 Forbes, "25 email etiquette rules that are worth of a reminder," Forbes, 29 September 2016. [Online]. Available: https://www.forbes.com/sites/dailymuse/2016/09/29/25-email-etiquette-rules-that-are-worthy-of-a-reminder/#10ad48442dd2. [Accessed 2018 September 10 2018].

67 A. Gingerich and T. T. Lineweaver, "OMG! Texting in class = U Fail :(Empirical evidence that text messaging during class disrupts comprehension," *Teaching of Psychology,* vol. 14, no. 1, pp. 44-51, January 2014.

68 R. Salem, "Empathic listening," July 2003. [Online]. Available: https://www.beyondintractability.org/essay/empathic_listening. [Accessed 20 August 2018].

69 A. Milofsky, "United States Institute of Peace: What is active listening?," [Online]. Available: https://www.usip.org/public-education/educators/what-active-listening. [Accessed 20 August 2018].

70 A. E. Quinn, "Effective communication in a time of connectivity: An interview with Dr. Beverly Helms," *The Delta Kappa Gamma Bulletin,* pp. 6-10, Spring 2014.

71 D. Shilling, "10 steps to effective listening," Forbes, 9 November 2012. [Online]. Available: https://www.forbes.com/sites/womensmedia/2012/11/09/10-steps-to-effective-listening/#5092b2d63891. [Accessed 15 August 2018].

72 A. Diaz-Uda, C. Medina and B. Schill, "Diversity of thought and the future of the workplace," 23 July 2013. [Online]. Available: https://www2.deloitte.com/insights/us/en/topics/talent/diversitys-new-frontier.html#endnote-sup-4.

73 R. Tulshyan, "Diversity of thought: What is it and why is it gaining so much traction?," [Online]. Available: http://www.diversitywoman.com/diversity-of-thought/. [Accessed 20 August 2018].

74 Princeton University, "Carebridge: Five steps to bridging the workforce generation gap," [Online]. Available:

75 https://www.princeton.edu/hr/benefits/pdf/generationgap.pdf. [Accessed 20 August 2018].

76 I. Bodker, "How baby boomer parents molded the millennial generation," Barkley, 15 August 215. [Online]. Available: https://www.barkleyus.com/insights/baby-boomer-parents-molded-millennial-generation/. [Accessed 4 September 2018].

77 M. Dimock, "Defining generatons: Where millennials end and post-millennials begin," Pew Research Center, 1 March 2018. [Online]. Available: http://www.pewresearch.org/fact-tank/2018/03/01/defining-generations-where-millennials-end-and-post-millennials-begin/. [Accessed 4 September 2018].

77 J. D. Baker, "The multigenerational perioperative nursing workforce: A celebration for Labor Day," *AORN Journal*, vol. 96, no. 3, pp. 231-234, September 2012.

78 A. Sawyer, "Communication styles differ with each generation," My Plainview, 22 September 2017. [Online]. Available: https://www.myplainview.com/news/article/Communication-styles-differ-with-each-generation-12220967.php. [Accessed 4 September 2018].

79 W. Liu, G. Pasman, J. Taal-Fokker and P. Stappers, "Exploring generation Y interaction qualities at home and at work," *Cognition, Technology and Work*, vol. 16, no. 3, pp. 405-415, 2014.

80 J. D. Baker, "Collaborative writing," *AORN Journal*, vol. 97, no. 1, pp. 4-6, 2013.

81 K. Boogaard, "Mixing millenials and baby boomers in the workplace melting pot," Officeninjas, [Online]. Available: https://officeninjas.com/mixing-millennials-and-baby-boomers-in-the-workplace-melting-pot/. [Accessed 20 August 2018].

82 J. O. Steen, "Bridging the generation gap through clear communication," *Tennessee Bar Journal*, no. April, pp. 3-4, 2015.

83. E. Venter, "Bridging the communication gap between generation Y and the baby boomer generation," *International Journal of Adolescence and Youth,* vol. 22, no. 4, pp. 497-507, 2017.
84. Vita Enterprise Solutions, "5 benefits of technology in business," 2018. [Online]. Available: https://vitaenterprisesolutions.com.au/new-ideas/articles/5-benefits-technology-business. [Accessed 22 August 2018].
85. A. Jay, "Harvard Business Review: How to run a meeting," March 1976. [Online]. Available: https://hbr.org/1976/03/how-to-run-a-meeting. [Accessed 22 August 2018].
86. Meetings.org, "Why have a meeting?," [Online]. Available: https://www.meetings.org/meeting1.htm. [Accessed 22 August 2018].
87. The Meeting Magazines, "Understanding the new purposeful meetings," 1 September 2017. [Online]. Available: http://www.themeetingmagazines.com/cit/understanding-new-purposeful-meetings/. [Accessed 22 August 2018].
88. W. Kim, A. M. Nicotera and J. McNulty, "Nurses' perceptions of conflict as constructive or destructive," *Journal of Advanced Nursing,* vol. 71, no. 9, p. 2073–2083, 2015.
89. S. Dmytriyev, R. E. Freeman and M. E. Haskins, "Transforming disagreements into opportunities to enhance learning, decision making and trust," *Strategy & Leadership,* vol. 44, no. 2, pp. 31-38, 2016.
90. C. Edmonson, B. Bolick and J. Lee, "A moral imperative for nurse leaders: Addressing incivility and bullying in health care," *Nurse Leader,* vol. 15, no. 1, p. 40–44, February 2017.
91. K. W. Thomas, "Making conflict management a strategic advantage," CPP, Inc. - The Myers-Briggs Company, Sunnyvale, CA, 2018.
92. N. Katz and K. McNulty, Conflict Resolution, Syracuse, NY: Syracuse University | Maxwell School, 1994.

93 P. Graham, Mary Parker Follett prophet of management, Frederick, Maryland: Beard Books, December 1, 2003.
94 M. P. Follett, Mary Parker Follett -- prophet of management: A celebration of writings from the 1920s, P. Graham, Ed., Boston, MA: Harvard Business School Press, 1995, p. 309.
95 R. Blake and J. Mouton, The managerial grid, Gulf Publishing Company, 1964.
96 The Partnership Resource, "Are you collaborating or compromising with your partner?," iris, 1 June 2018. [Online]. Available: https://www.iris.xyz/partnerships/are-you-collaborating-or-compromising-your-partner. [Accessed 5 September 2018].
97 W. Lin, Y. Lin, C. Huang and L. Chen, "We can make it better: "We" moderates the relationship between a compromising style in interpersonal conflict and well-being," *Journal of Happiness Studies,* vol. 17, pp. 41-57, 2016.
98 S. Ahmed and H. Mohammad, "Gender differences in intimate relationships: Sacrifice and compromise," *FWU Journal of Social Sciences,* vol. 7 No 1, no. Summer, pp. 57-60, 2013.
99 S. Covey, The 7 Habits of Highly Effective People, New York, NY: Simon & Schuster, 1989.
100 P. Kiplagat, M. Atieno and E. Mboya, "Collaboration conflict management strategy: A solution to secondary schools' unrests in Kenya," *International Journal of Trend in Research and Development,* vol. 3, pp. 203-207, January 20016.
101 S. Quain, "The advantages & disadvantages of collaborating conflict management," Small Business-Chron.com, 27 June 2018. [Online]. Available: https://smallbusiness.chron.com/advantages-disadvantages-collaborating-conflict-management-36052.html. [Accessed 5 September 2018].
102 K. Patterson, Crucial conversations: Tools for talking when stakes are high, K. Patterson, Ed., New York: McGraw-Hill, 2012.

[103] M. S. Hershcovis, L. Neville, T. C. Reich, A. M. Christie, L. M. Cortinae and J. V. Shan, "The effects of observer power on incivility intervention in the workplace," *Organizational Behavior and Human Decision Processes*, vol. 142, pp. 45-57, 2017.

[104] S. Dmytriyev, R. E. Freeman and M. E. Haskins, "Transforming disagreements into opportunities to enhance learning, decision making and trust," *Strategy & Leadership*, vol. 44, no. 2, pp. 31-38, 2016.

[105] P. Gleeson, "Five approaches to conflict resolution," Small Business-chron.com, 29 June 2018. [Online]. Available: http://smallbusiness.chron.com/five-approaches-conflict-resolution-21360.html. [Accessed 5 September 2018].

[106] M. S. Rao, "Tools and techniques to resolve organizational conflicts amicably," *Industrial and Commercial Training*, vol. 49, no. 2, pp. 93-97, 2017.

[107] American Marketing Association, "American Marketing Association," 2013. [Online]. Available: https://www.ama.org/AboutAMA/Pages/Definition-of-Marketing.aspx. [Accessed 30 August 2018].

[108] S. M. Resnick, R. Cheng, M. Simpson and F. Lourenço, "Marketing in SMEs: a "4Ps" self-branding model," *International Journal of Entrepreneurial Behavior & Research*, vol. 22, no. 1, pp. 155-174, 2016.

[109] N. H. Borden, "The concept of the marketing mix," *Journal of Advertising Research*, vol. 4, pp. 2-7, 1964.

[110] E. J. McCarthy, Basic marketing: A management approach, Homewood, IL: Richard D. Irwin, 1960.

[111] S. Dann and S. Dann, "Insight and overview of insight and overview of social marketing," Government of Qeensland, Australia, 2011.

[112] A. Kareh, "Evolution of the four Ps: Revisiting the marketing mix," 3 January 2018. [Online]. Available: https://www.forbes.com/sites/forbesagencycouncil/2018/01/03/evolution-of-the-four-ps-revisitin

[113] g-the-marketing-mix/#643c81d81120. [Accessed 30 August 2018].

[113] R. F. Lauterborn, "New marketing litany: Four P's passé; C-words take over," 1 October 1990. [Online]. Available: http://rlauterborn.com/pubs/pdfs/4_Cs.pdf. [Accessed 30 August 2018].

[114] K. Q. Dadzie, D. K. Amponsah, C. A. Dadzie and E. M. Winston, "How firms implement marketing strategies in emerging markets: An empirical assessment of the 4A marketing mix framework," *Journal of Marketing Theory and Practice,* vol. 25, no. 3, pp. 234-256, Summer 2017.

[115] J. N. Sheth and R. Sisodia, The 4 A's of marketing, Milton Park, Abingon / Oxfordshire: Routledge, 2011.

[116] statista: The Statistics Portal, "E-book sales as a percentage of total book sales worldwide in 2013 and 2018," statista, 2018. [Online]. Available: https://www.statista.com/statistics/234106/e-book-market-share-worldwide/. [Accessed 5 September 2018].

[117] A. Conrad, "Understanding the marketing Mix: the 4P's of marketing," Capterra Sales and Marketing Tech Blog, 27 September 2017. [Online]. Available: https://blog.capterra.com/understanding-the-marketing-mix-the-4-ps-of-marketing/. [Accessed 5 September 2018].

[118] J. Artale, "10 trends driving the future of publishing," Alliance of Independent Authors, 30 August 2016. [Online]. Available: https://selfpublishingadvice.org/10-trends-driving-the-future-of-publishing-podcast-with-mark-coker/. [Accessed 5 September 2018].

[119] Goodreads, "Meet your next favorite book," Goodreads, Inc., [Online]. Available: https://www.goodreads.com/. [Accessed 11 September 2018].

[120] Northwestern University Spiegel Research Center, "How online reviews influence sales," June 2017. [Online]. Available: http://spiegel.medill.northwestern.edu/_pdf/

Spiegel_Online%20Review_eBook_Jun2017_FINAL.pdf. [Accessed 30 August 2018].

[121] marketingmix.co.uk, "The marketing mix: Definition of the 4P's and 7P's," [Online]. Available: http://marketingmix.co.uk. [Accessed 30 August 2018].

[122] M. N. Anwar and E. Daniel, "Entrepreneurial marketing in online businesses: The case of ethnic minority entrepreneurs in the UK," *Qualitative Market Research: An International Journal,* vol. 19, no. 3, pp. 310-338, 2016.

[123] R. G. Duffett, "Influence of social media marketing communications on young consumers' attitudes," *Young Consumers,* vol. 18, no. 1, pp. 19-39, 2017.

[124] R. Cheng, F. Lourenço and S. Resnick, "Educating graduates for marketing in SMEs: An update for the traditional marketing curriculum," *Journal of Small Business and Enterprise Development,* vol. 23, no. 2, pp. 495-513, 2016.

[125] N. Patel, "If I had to start a blog from scratch, I would…," [Online]. Available: https://neilpatel.com/blog/blogging-principles/?utm_source=email&utm_medium=email&utm_campaign=email. [Accessed 29 November 2018].

[126] S. Abdallah and B. Jaleel, "Website appeal: Development of an assessment tool and evaluation framework of e-marketing," vol. 10, no. 3, pp. 45-62, September 2015.

[127] K. Reinecke, T. Yeh, L. Miratrix, R. Mardiko, Y. Zhao, L. J. and K. Z. Gajos, "Predicting users' first impressions of website aesthetics with a quantification of perceived visual complexity and colorfulness," in *Proceedings of the SIGCHI Conference on Human Factors in Computing Systems,* New York, 2013.

[128] BigCommerce, "Effective social media use in eCommerce marketing," [Online]. Available: https://www.bigcommerce.com/ecommerce-answers/effective-social-media-use-ecommerce-marketing/. [Accessed 30 August 2018].

129. F. Hiss, "Talk, time, and creativity: Developing ideas and identities during a start-up weekend," *Language & Communication,* vol. 60, no. 01, pp. 64-79, 2018.

130. S. Greenberg, "The ethics of narrative: A return to the source.," *Journalism,* vol. 15, no. 5, pp. 517-532, 2014.

131. W. Dick and L. Carey, "Learning theories: ADDIE model," [Online]. Available: https://www.learning-theories.com/addie-model.html. [Accessed 3 May 2018].

132. R. Culatta, "ADDIE Model," 2018. [Online]. Available: http://www.instructionaldesign.org/models/addie/. [Accessed 8 June 2018].

133. J. Ferriman, "ADDIE cheat sheet - LearnDash," 18 February 2014. [Online]. Available: https://www.learndash.com/addie-cheat-sheet/. [Accessed 8 Jun 2018].

134. C. Gilkey, "Stand tall, creative giants.," 23 January 2014. [Online]. Available: https://www.productiveflourishing.com/creative-giants/?__s=dmxtqi2tqkoti2j5w1oy&utm_source=drip&utm_medium=email&utm_campaign=Productive+Flourishing+Free+Resource+Tour&utm_content=%5BProductive+Flourishing%5D+Welcome+to+the+Productive+Flourishing+Communit. [Accessed 8 June 2018].

135. N. Kim, "Critical thinking in wikibook creation with enhanced and minimal scaffolds.," *Education Tech Research Dev,* vol. 63, pp. 5-33, 2015.

136. L. Scott, "Digging deep: Self-study as a reflexive approach to improving my practice as an artist, researcher, and teacher," *Persepctives in Education,* vol. 32, no. 2, pp. 69-88, 2014.

137. J. Katz-Buonincontro, "Implications of Kant's theories of art for developing creative identity in students," *Journal of Aesthetic Education,* vol. 49, no. 4, pp. 1-18, 2015.

138. D. R. Bell, "Learning, play, and creativity: Asobi, Suzuki Harunobu, and the creative practice," *The Journal of Aesthetic Education,* vol. 50, no. 4, pp. 86-113, 2016.

ACKNOWLEDGEMENTS

Every book is similar to a new baby who needs a village to support its successful growth and development. Our sincere thank you to beta readers who took time to provide us detailed feedback and helped to make the book valuable a resource. Dr. Jennifer Gray, Dr. Kathy Gaberson, Dr. Nancy Girard, Dr. Jane Rothrock, and Ms. Patricia Seifert provided significant expertise and editorial support and guidance as we developed the book. Additionally, we acknowledge Amy Clark, Chelsie Gable, Greg Goodman, and Daryn Harrington, who reviewed our book and provided content and copy editing throughout the process.

Icons from *PresenterMedia* introduce each chapter. We are grateful to have worked with talented individuals and companies who supported our work, providing cover design (*Fresh Design*), interior design (*jetlaunch.net*), and printing (*Vervante*). We owe a debt of gratitude to our family and friends who allow us to stay focused on writing and advancing the mission of the book.

AUTHOR NOTES

While we use brand names to illustrate examples of programs. We do not receive funding for any software or products mentioned. We have either used the products ourselves or perceive there is value in them for our readers.

We are not attorneys. No content in this book is to be construed as legal advice. Seek an attorney for any legal advice required.

Please visit https://www.bakergoodman.com and join our mailing list for notification of new releases. *Friend us* on Facebook at Baker & Goodman Nurseketeers Authors, http://www.facebook.com/jt.bakergoodman, and follow our Author page, https://www.facebook.com/bakergoodmanbooks, or email us at admin@bakergoodman.com.

Please post a review on Amazon regarding our book. We welcome and tremendously value your feedback.

ABOUT THE AUTHORS

Joy Don Baker, *PhD, RN-BC, CNOR, CNE, NEA-BC, FAAN* and Terri Goodman, *PhD, RN, CNOR as* writing partners have also co-authored *The Wake-Up Call,* the first novel in the *Nurseketeers Series.* Their second book in the series is scheduled for publication in 2019. They are both accomplished authors, speakers at national and international conferences, and leaders in perioperative nursing.

Dr. Baker has served as the Editor-in-Chief of the *AORN Journal* and on the national AORN Board of Directors as director and vice president. Baker received the *Outstanding Achievement in Perioperative Academic Nursing Education* award. She is a Clinical Professor at The University of Texas at Arlington where she teaches Evidence-Based Practice in the nursing masters' program.

Dr. Goodman is the owner and CEO of Terri Goodman & Associates, an Approved Provider of continuing nursing education, and was a recipient of AORN's *Jerry G. Peers Outstanding Service Award.*

www.ingramcontent.com/pod-product-compliance
Lightning Source LLC
Chambersburg PA
CBHW071346080526
44587CB00017B/2991